William Gibson

Paris During the Commune

William Gibson

Paris During the Commune

ISBN/EAN: 9783337429126

Printed in Europe, USA, Canada, Australia, Japan

Cover: Foto ©ninafisch / pixelio.de

More available books at **www.hansebooks.com**

PARIS
DURING THE COMMUNE,

By REV. W. GIBSON,

WITH A CHARACTER SKETCH BY HIS WIFE.

London:
METHODIST BOOK ROOM, CASTLE STREET, CITY ROAD,
AND PATERNOSTER ROW.

Nottingham:
HOWITT AND SON, PRINTERS, CLUMBER STREET.

1895.

WILLIAM GIBSON

OF PARIS.

A

CHARACTER SKETCH.

I

What can I say about one of the brightest, purest, loveliest spirits that ever sojourned for a while on this earth?

As I write, solemn influences from his last moments still linger round me, and it seems almost desecration to make public any details concerning one whose life was signalized by humility and self-forgetfulness. But I would fain have him live on longer here below than will even the tenderest memories of those who loved him best. Being dead, I would have him yet speak, and speak to the glory of the God he loved and served from childhood.

I feel convinced that the simple portrayal of a character such as his cannot fail to prove an inspiration to some who will henceforth seek to follow him as he followed Christ.

As to my own pain in recalling so many hallowed but now harrowing memories I count it a very small offering to bring for over thirty-two years of incomparable devotion and almost infinite tenderness, and the sad satisfaction outweighs the suffering. His family are not alone in appreciating his singular worth: over four hundred beautiful letters recently received bear unqualified testimony to his faultless life, his ideally perfect character and his wide-spread and holy influence. From all parts of the world witnesses rise up to call him blessed, in that he not only pointed them to the way of life but by his own Christlike example helped them to walk in it.

He " lived with God in such untroubled love,
And clear confiding, as a child on whom
The Father's face has never yet but smiled;

And with men even, in such harmony
Of brotherhood, that whatsoever spark
Of pure and true in any human heart
Flickered and lived, it burned itself towards him."

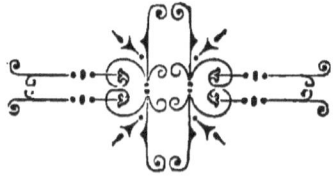

Whosoever shall not receive the kingdom of God as a little child shall in no wise enter therein. (Luke xviii., 17.)

Oh! say not, dream not, heavenly notes
    To childish ears are vain,
That the young mind at random floats,
    And cannot reach the strain.

Dim or unheard, the words may fall,
    And yet the heaven-taught mind
May learn the sacred airs, and all
    The harmony unwind.

    *   *   *   *   *

Child-like though the voices be
    And untuneable the parts,
Thou wilt own the minstrelsy,
    If it flow from child-like hearts.

Who but a Christian, through all life
    That blessing may prolong?
Who, thro' the world's sad day of strife,
    Still chant his morning song?

Keble.

II

William Gibson was brought to understand the love of God at the age of 11. I give the account in his own words, taken from a letter in the memoir of Joseph B. Shrewsbury, who was his intimate friend and the means of his conversion :—

"Wesley College, Dec. 8, 1849.

In the summer of 1843 I went to Woodhouse Grove School, and as it is always more pleasant, and also more safe, to have some senior boy to take a little oversight of boys just entering upon their school life, my brother John, who had contracted a friendship with Joseph at the Grove, thought it well to write a few lines to him requesting him to look after me a little.

As soon as Joseph arrived I handed him this letter, and he, thinking, as he told me afterwards, that the best way to look after me was to lead me to Christ, took me by the arm in the play-ground, and began to talk to me about my soul.

I had been seriously inclined for some time previous, so that I was quite ready and willing to receive and to attend to all he said. We went together to the footstool of mercy, and he directed me to "the Lamb of God which taketh away the sin of the world." I continued in this state of repentance two days, during which he spent nearly the whole of the play hours in praying beside me, and leading me to Christ. After these two days, at the prayer-meeting, at five o'clock in the afternoon, when I was standing beside him endeavouring to assist in singing, "Praise God from whom all blessings flow," &c., because one of our school-fellows had been brought into the glorious liberty of the children of God, the Lord revealed Himself to me as my Saviour, and thus burst the bonds which held my spirit in thraldom, causing me to rejoice in the unclouded smile of my reconciled Father.

Then began a *Christian* friendship between us, which being so suddenly terminated upon earth will, I trust, be consummated in heaven."

A week after his conversion he began to keep a journal. I have the first little document before me now. Two sheets of small note-paper folded in half and covered with a bit of thin green cardboard, the whole carefully protected by a piece of school-report paper on which is inscribed in a good round hand :

*I forbid anyone
to look within.
Private.*

Wm. Gibson.

"Within" is a touching record of a child's walk with God, a walk even then assured and steadfast, and which became steadier and straighter the further he walked until the day that "he was not, for God took him." Truly the child was father to the man. From the very first full salvation for himself and for all around him was the absorbing desire of his soul, constraining him to give up the larger part of his play-time to prayer.

Friday, July 7, 1843, was the date of his conversion, and I think he never forgot the anniversary. He always spoke of it as being literally to him a new birth—a complete transformation of all his tastes, desires and tempers. But we had hard work to believe he ever could have been anything but perfect. Does not this prove the inestimable value of *early* conversion ?

"I heard the voice of the Lord, saying, whom shall I send, and who will go for us? Then said I, here am I, send me." (Isa. vi. 8).

"If two of you shall agree on earth, as touching anything that they shall ask, it shall be done for them of my father which is in heaven." (Matt. xviii. 19).

"Call unto me, and I will answer thee, and shew thee great and mighty things that thou knowest not." (Jer. xxiii. 3).

" Let not fine culture, poesy, art, sweet tones,
Build up about my soothèd sense a world
That is not Thine and wall me up in dreams ;
So my sad heart may cease to pulse with Thine,
The great world-Heart, whose blood, for ever shed,
Is human life, whose ache is man's dull pain.
Let not my grasp on Life's most awful Truth
Be loosened ; but where'er the people hear
Quick-eared, as closer unto life, Thy step,
And thronging bring their dumb hearts unto Thee,
To ease the ache that has no easeful words,
There, through all rudest speech and gestures mean,
Obscuring sights, and harsh fanatic sounds,
Still may I see the Christ in faded vesture ;
Nor stand with Greeks and coldly criticise
The mean apparel, in whose tarnished hem,
By a diviner instinct led, the lost,
The sad, the poor, the sinful find sweet healing.
                                    Ellice Hopkins.

III.

When only 15 William Gibson decided to follow in his father's steps and be a Christian minister, and from that moment he devoted all his energies to preparing himself mentally and spiritually for what he held to be one of the highest and holiest of all callings.

From the very first he had a passion for souls.

He was one of the five lads who in 1848 banded together at Wesley College to pray for a revival in the place. The result was glorious. He wrote an account of the blessed "three days," which I print *in toto*, trusting that it may be suggestive to the present generation of lads at school.

" At the beginning of the "second half," 1848, five youths, who alone among the boys then at Wesley College, professed to live in the enjoyment of religion, *i.e.*, to have communion with God as their Father and to rest in the assurance of His love to them, resolved to appoint a time to pray specially for the outpouring of the Spirit upon the school. Accordingly, seven o'clock on Saturday evening was fixed for this special prayer meeting, and the little band met regularly in the vestry adjoining the College Chapel for this particular purpose. Pleading earnestly and importunately " whatsoever two of you shall agree on earth, as touching anything that they shall ask, it shall be done for them of my Father which is in heaven," those five became assured that God heard and would answer their prayers. That room, while they thus wrestled with the Angel of the Covenant, was to them none other than the house of God. The heavens were opened; the place was filled with the Divine glory, and each was overwhelmed with a sense of the immediate presence of God.

One Saturday, earnest supplications were offered on behalf of those boys who, as it appeared, were the least likely to be converted, and special mention of them was made by name.

On the following Tuesday, one of the five proposed a special prayer meeting in the vestry, to plead again for the outpouring of the Spirit. The proposition was at once eagerly embraced; and the five boys on that day again united to implore the descent of the Holy Ghost.

On Wednesday morning, November 22nd, at six o'clock, one of the college boys (Bealey) exchanged time for eternity. He had been ill for some time; and general interest had been aroused in his behalf. The first question each morning for a fortnight had been " How is Bealey?" The hearts of all were saddened as they heard each day that he was worse.

After breakfast on that Wednesday morning the Governor detained the boys: it was evident from his countenance that he had something sad to communicate. After a brief pause, he told us that at six o'clock Bealey had breathed his last; but that he had left us a glorious testimony,—that he had expressed his assurance of his interest in the blood of Christ, and that he was going home to heaven.

The Governor, the Rev. Samuel D. Waddy, was evidently powerfully affected. He proceeded, as soon as his feelings would allow him, to address an earnest exhortation to the boys, on the importance of personal religion and preparation for death. I have heard him speak hundreds of times but never with such power as on that morning. The boys were without exception moved to tears; there was not a dry eye throughout the school. He must have had a hard heart indeed who could have resisted the force of the earnest and persuasive appeal that fell from the Governor's lips.

The address was concluded by an announcement that there would be a prayer meeting that morning at twelve o'clock. By five minutes past twelve the vestry, which had ordinarily been quite large enough for the prayer meetings, was filled; the steps leading down from the music room were crowded, and numbers, unable to gain admission were standing in the music room above. It was necessary to adjourn into the chapel. There were not twenty boys absent, out of the hundred and sixty. The Governor, on entering the play ground between twelve and one, was surprised to find it deserted; but his surprise was changed to joy, when one of his family came running to him with the cry " Oh ! do come into the chapel.'' Eight out of the number at the prayer meeting appeared to be earnestly seeking salvation. They were, accordingly invited to a meeting to be held in the vestry at half-past two o'clock. Eight more would force their way into the vestry, notwithstanding efforts made to exclude them lest they should have come only " to make fun." They were, however, all true penitents ! The power of the Spirit was present to heal the broken heart. One after another was made happy in the love of Christ; and, about four o'clock, we sang a hearty hallelujah for sixteen souls passed from darkness unto light.

As we came up from the prayer meeting we were met by others, asking with tearful eyes why they were not invited, for they were indeed in earnest. In half an hour the vestry was filled again with seekers of salvation. The music room was also crowded with penitents; and there was a general cry, " What must I do to be saved ?" At eight o'clock in the evening, one of the boys for whom special intercession had been offered the previous Saturday, and who, on hearing of the general concern manifested by the boys for salvation, had been inclined to treat the whole with contempt, was reading a novel in his room. From some indefinable and unaccountable influence over his mind he was unable to read. At last, a voice seemed to say to him, Go to the prayer meeting. He closed the novel and went to the door of the room. " What a fool I am going to make of myself," he said, and went back to his desk and took up his novel; but he was unable to read. Another inward struggle and he was a second time at the door of his room. With a second exclamation similar to the first, he returned a third time to his book. Still he was uneasy; there was a perfect tumult within : flinging the book down and desperately forcing himself away, he hastened through the covered play-ground where no one could observe him, to the door of the vestry. His heart failed him, and he hurried back to his room. He opened his book ; but he could not compel his eyes to trace its pages. Unable to control his agitated spirit, and overwhelmed with the power of conviction he rushed out of his room, made his way quickly to the vestry, threw open the door, and without waiting to close it, flung himself, a weeping penitent, upon his knees beside one of the forms. That very night he stepped into the glorious liberty of the children of God. Before we retired to the dormitories seventy-five of the boys had tasted that the Lord is gracious, and could rejoice in the forgiveness of sin. In each bedroom a prayer meeting was held till near midnight. Many could not sleep that night for gladness of heart.

On Thursday, the 23rd, two of the masters who had not been living in the enjoyment of religion began to seek the pearl of great price; several of the servants were deeply convinced of sin, and at the evening prayer meeting three or four of them passed into the glorious freedom of the gospel.

Prayer meetings were constantly held in the chapel vestry and school rooms during out-of-school hours, and many more believed with the heart unto righteousness. The whole building was filled with the voice of prayer and praise. One youth at the evening prayer meeting in the vestry was in a great agony of supplication; his whole frame betokened the severity of the struggle going on within. He literally writhed in agony of soul, groaning out in the bitterness of his spirit, "God be merciful to me a sinner." He wrestled on till his knees were sore; but so determined was he not to be content without a conviction of the pardoning mercy of God, that he expressed the resolve not to stir from that place till he could rejoice in God as his reconciled Father. "The Kingdom of Heaven suffereth violence; and the violent take it by force." He soon heard the whisper of peace—"Thy sins which are many are all forgiven thee."

The Governor was accustomed to meet a class on Thursday evening. Twenty or thirty in attendance had been a large number, but now a hundred and thirty were wishful to be present. The Governor, therefore, as it was impossible for him to speak to each individually, delivered a pointed address to us collectively in the chapel, and concluded with a prayer meeting. The masters were present, but they took no part in the meeting. The boys alone engaged in prayer. From the lips of youths, not accustomed to pray, supplications, consecutive in thought and beautiful in language, were poured forth in a continuous torrent of earnest and prevailing prayer. Such prayers I had never heard before—such prayers I have never heard since. It seemed as though they were inspired. Ours was truly the gladness of a full heart, and the joy of a loosened tongue.

The bedrooms that night all became rooms for prayer; and importunate supplications were prolonged far into the night.

The question on the Friday, November the 24th, was not Who are saved? but Who are *not* converted? and intercessory supplications were offered for those who still remained without a saving interest in Christ. The laboratory, the music room, the reading room, the school rooms, and the students' rooms, were all occupied with knots of earnest pleaders at the Throne of Grace. A few went into the play-ground; but—the football lying untouched on the grass—they paced the grounds, arm-in-arm, singing—

" Glory, honour, praise, and power,
    Be unto the Lamb for ever :
Jesus Christ is our Redeemer ;
    Hallelujah, &c.

The prayer meeting on the Friday evening will never be forgotten by any who were present. All were filled with the
" Speechless awe that dares not move,
    And all the silent heaven of love."

The influence in the College chapel that night was iterally overpowering. All alike *felt*
" Lo, God is here ! Let all adore
    And own how dreadful is this place."

It became generally known that there was only one boy in the whole school unconverted ; and all were drawn out in prayer that his heart might be subdued. One of the five who had prayed from the beginning of the half year for the outpouring of the Spirit, went up from the prayer meeting to induce if possible this last boy, who remained careless and unconcerned, to come down into the chapel. He found him sitting by himself in one of the school rooms, but could not move him by solicitations. " Will you allow me to pray with you ?" " You may pray if you like, but I shall put my fingers in my ears." (Our readers will be glad to know that even this rebellious spirit yielded to the love of God some years later)." He returned to the chapel, and as he entered the doors, so powerful was his emotion, and so deep his concern on behalf of the only impenitent boy in the whole school, that he was trembling from head to foot. He laid hold of my arm to prevent himself from falling, and I could feel that his whole frame was tremulous with intensity of emotion. The songs of praise in all the bedrooms that night were surely " such as angels sing." It was truly Heaven begun below.

Eleven years have passed away ; but those three days are as fresh in my recollection as though they had transpired last week. They have not ceased to exert their influence upon me to this day. And many a time has my heart been cheered by living them over again in memory.

There were two remarkable characteristics of this revival of religion.

One was the entire absence of human agency. If the masters were present, they only came *silently* to enjoy the sacred and hallowed influence. The five boys who had been in the school phrase "religious" previously, did not take any lead ; they only prayed in turn with the rest. They who directed the penitent to the cross were those who had themselves just proved that Christ hath power on earth to forgive sins. It was not by might nor power, but by the Spirit of the Lord.

The other peculiar characteristic was an entire absence of noise or excitement. There were no loud Amens,—no shouting,—no confusion. Not that we would condemn loud manifestations of *sincere* religious feeling (let the Lord work as he wills!) ; but a sacred quietness was the peculiarity of this revival. " The wind bloweth where it listeth ; and thou hearest the sound thereof, but canst not tell whence it cometh, and whither it goeth."

" But have they remained steadfast?" " What has been the permanent result ?

" These questions can be answered satisfactorily :—

(1) Although fifty, nearly one-third of the whole number, left at the end of the half year, the influence of the revival remained throughout the following year, nor has it ceased to this day to exert a gracious power, for traditions of this remarkable work still linger in the College, and the recital of its circumstances still stimulates the religious feelings of the boys.

(2) As to the steadfastness of those who were converted. There have been some backsliders ; *but fewer than in any revival of which I have heard or read.* Some who were then converted have exchanged mortality for life. Some have become active members of the Methodist Society. Some have joined other denominations of Christ's church, and occupy, in various parts of the great vineyard, positions of honour and usefulness.

(3) Numbers have been converted through the instrumentality of those who were then brought to a knowledge of the truth. Two revivals—one at Crookes, one at Ratcliffe—resulted immediately, from simply hearing of the glorious news. Many cases might be given in which the mere recital of these never-to-be-forgotten scenes in different towns in England, and 'afar off' in foreign lands, has led to deep concern for salvation. One instance could be cited in which, while listening to an account of this revival, given in a town in the south of England, two were then and there led to Christ. All the good that has resulted and will result from this memorable revival cannot be known till the ' books ' are ' opened.'

The writer trusts that the perusal of this imperfect sketch of one of the most remarkable effusions of the Spirit ever vouchsafed to a seminary of learning, may lead the boys now at Wesley College to pray for a like baptism of the Holy Ghost.

The thought of publishing the above account was partly suggested by reading of the revivals in Ireland. Why should there not be in every school a revival such as that with which Wesley College was blessed in 1848 ! We have the same God, equally faithful to his promises ; His 'ear' not 'heavy ;' His ' arm ' not ' shortened.'

How is such a revival in any place to be ensured? Let a few earnest believers meet together for the special purpose of interceding with God on behalf of the ungodly. Let them not be satisfied until their prayers are answered. Let them give God no rest day or night until He grant the gift of the Holy Ghost, and 'pour floods upon the dry ground."

'O wondrous power of faithful prayer!
What tongue can tell the Almighty grace?
God's hands or bound or open are,
As Moses or Elijah prays.'

Let them mention before the Lord, in their united supplications, the names of lukewarm professors, and of the most notorious sinners. The *certain* consequence will be the outpouring of the spirit.

Assuredly the expected revival will come. 'The times of refreshing from the presence of the Lord' are at hand.'"

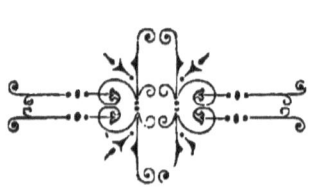

The law of his God is in his heart, none of his steps shall slide. (Pro. 37, 31.)

Be thou an example of the believers, in word, in conversation, in charity, in spirit, in faith, in purity. (I. Tim. iv., 12.)

If in the paths of the world
Stones might have wounded thy feet,
Toil or dejection have tried
Thy spirit, of that we saw
Nothing—to us thou wast still
Cheerful and helpful and firm!
Therefore to thee it was given
Many to save with thyself.

Matthew Arnold.

IV.

Wordsworth says :—
" 'Tis the most difficult of tasks to keep
Heights which the soul is competent to gain."
William Gibson not only gained those heights, but kept them, and drew other struggling souls up to them.

Lives like his are the great want of the world. Passionate pleaders, ready reasoners, and earnest expositors abound in the pulpit and out of it, but Christ-like men, epistles of Christ, are rare anywhere. Men out of whose eyes Christ looks, through whose lips Christ speaks, and whose every act is a reminder of Christ—what a small sprinkling is there of such throughout Christendom!

My husband was permeated with the Spirit of Christ, so that his preaching and his practice agreed. He did not pull down with one hand what he had built up with the other, as is always done when a man's teaching and temper are at variance. A talented talker may make nominal Christians, but only a saintly soul can make saints. While my husband's bright cheerfulness attracted outsiders toward the religion of Christ, his singular consistency tended to confirm them in it. Thank God, I do not believe he was ever an occasion of stumbling to anyone.

Almost immediately after his conversion he became deeply interested in the subject of holiness. When yet a child at school the eyes of his understanding were enlightened to know what is the exceeding greatness of God's power to those who believe. He trusted that power and found it avail.

His humility was as genuine as his faith was simple and tenacious. He always felt himself to be only a sinner saved by Almighty grace, but he knew that he was saved, and gave God the glory. His ideas of entire sanctification were very practical; he loved to speak of it as a life obligatory on each Christian, and he could speak with authority of a life he himself lived. Full trust in Christ as a Saviour from all sin, and a daily renewed experience of the Spirit's regenerating influences, sufficed to keep him from falling in the midst oft-times of annoyances and aggravations that were a severe test. He had put on "the ornament of a meek and quiet spirit, which is in the sight of God of *great price.*"

And verily the meek do inherit the earth, and may delight themselves in the abundance of peace! His exquisite gentleness and patience not only called forth the almost adoration of his family and household, but also very generally secured him his own way, for none of us ever had the heart to withstand him.

His favourite hymns treated of the Atonement and of the boundless love of God in Christ. Night after night did he soothe himself to sleep with "How do Thy mercies close me round," or "For ever here my rest shall be." This precious little hymn comforted his last hours upon earth.

He may be equalled by many, and surpassed by some, in learning and in genius, but in hard, persevering, energetic work-capacity, in high-souled devotion, in sublime unselfishness and goodness (God-likeness), William Gibson stands out head and shoulders above most of his generation.

It can truly be said of him he was always "in the Spirit;" prayer was his native air; he never felt it out of place to pray. Whether in the midst of discussing some knotty, annoying mission question, or whether enjoying a hearty laugh over a humorous story, he would stop in an instant, if required, and go down on his knees with as much fervour and evident pleasure as though he were in a church. He had early formed the blessed habit of rising betimes for prayer and Bible-reading. It was in these quiet morning hours, alone with God, that he gained the strength to persevere in his difficult work ; it was then that he formed plans and projects for the mission, to be carried out with the dogged perseverance that so characterized him, long after the primal inspiration had died away.

His "tasks in hours of insight willed"
Were oft " thro' hours of gloom fulfilled."

When quite a lad he wrote a list, which I have since found in his early journal, of subjects for daily private prayer. The list begins with his step-mother, contains every possible relation near or distant, and ends up with ministers and missionaries. This habit of detail in prayer, as distinguished from the wholesale style one is so prone to adopt in this busy age, continued with him to the last.

Every morning before leaving his room he would pray with me for each member of the family on both sides, his and mine, and very often by name—brothers, sisters, nieces, nephews, none were forgotten.

The last sentence in his last report is a prayer—a prayer for blessing upon all his helpers and for the speedy conversion of his beloved France. As we were preparing the report he remarked that it was probably the last we should draw up together, and doubtless it was in view of the proposed changes that he felt the timeliness of prayer. All his stations were begun and continued in prayer. Havre, Honfleur, Rouen and Elbeuf, St. Malo, Boulogne, Chantilly, Asnières, and St. Cloud, together with the other halls in and around Paris, how importunately have they all been borne up before God! As for Rouen, I "testify that I have seen" when I speak of hours at one stretch spent on his knees in intercession for that station.

He believed in Methodism as a perfect piece of machinery, a gigantic and magnificent steam engine, able to run as well in France as in England or America; capable, indeed, of bearing along the whole world, *if fired by the Holy Ghost*. Therefore the burden of his prayers was always for a renewed *Pentecost*.

Ought a mission, begun and brought up to its present point by unceasing prayer, untiring energy, and consummate self-sacrifice, to be subjected to *retrenchment* as soon as its founder is laid in his grave? And yet so must it be unless help comes in voluntarily.

"The thoughts of the diligent tend only to plenteousness." (Prov. xxi., 5.)

" Be . . . . . not slothful in business, fervent in spirit, serving the Lord." (Rom. xii., 11.)

" It is more blessed to give than to receive." (Acts xx., 35.)

There is that that maketh himself poor, yet hath great riches." (Prov. xiii., 7.)

Measure thy life by loss instead of gain,
Not by the wine drunk, but the wine poured forth.
For love's strength standeth in love's sacrifice,
And whoso suffers most hath most to give.
H. E. H. King.

So others shall take patience, labour to their heart and hand

From thy hand, and thy heart, and thy brave cheer;
And God's grace fructify through thee to all.
E. B. Browning.

V.

Service for others was the law of my husband's life. On the principle of " No deed too little for great love to do " he stooped to the merest trifles in the way of small attentions to all around him. No press of business made him thoughtless of other people's feelings, nor absent-minded when it was a question of their comfort; neither did he mar a courteous act by making a merit of it. Therefore was it that he always avoided seeming hurried to visitors and conveying the impression that he had not a minute to spare. In his bureau at Rue Roquépine he would put aside the most important correspondence to receive a succession of callers with the ease and cordiality of a gentleman at leisure, and then write half through the night to regain the time. His strict punctuality and his habit of obliging, at any cost, each day to do its own work, alone enabled him to get through the incredible amount of business that fell to his lot.

With him everything was subservient to *duty*. Duty first, pleasure afterwards, was his watchword. But if pleasure had not graciously come to meet him in duty, he would not have seen much of her in this life.

He loved spiritual work; preaching, holding prayer and class meetings, whatever was of a purely soul-saving character was his special delight; and yet during his last 16 years his chief occupations were organizing, " serving tables," collecting.

His great practical difficulty arose from the lack of funds for the Mission. He could not keep within the committee's grant, believing, as he did, that it was " now or never " for spreading an undiluted Gospel throughout

France. Therefore he felt forced to collect, but there is no doubt the terribly fatiguing travelling late and early, the trudging from one end of a town to another in all weathers, and the sleepless nights spent in writing to the persons he had failed to find, hastened his end.

Collecting was to him the most utterly uncongenial and distasteful of the many disagreeable things he had to do. Repulsed nine times out of ten, disheartened, wearied—both bodily and mentally—he suffered enough at such times to rub the bloom off the ripest spirituality, but his only thrived " the more exceedingly." Often has he told me of the blessed peace and strengthening communion with God realized by him in some of his most discouraging collecting tours. In his hands the secular work never clashed with the spiritual, for he held that a man needed to be full of faith and of the Holy Ghost to do either well. He lived *with*, he lived *in* God, and his piety had the freshness and vigour of its Divine source, and pervaded whatever he undertook.

And after all, there were two sides to the collecting question. I must pay a tribute here to the kindness and liberality of the many friends who, during these several years, have kept the Mission going by their gifts, and who have so often and so hospitably entertained the collector. His daily letters used to be filled with the goodness of the various ministers and laymen who received him into their houses and cheered and lightened his toils by their sympathy and help.

My husband had strong intellectual tastes; philosophy was his hobby. He never went anywhere without books, which explains in part our manifold and bulky packages in travelling. He used to say he liked to have me with him as I got the credit of the unreasonable number of handbags! Once when a fastidious Frenchman protested against our undue appropriation of the compartment, and my sense of justice inclined me to side with him, my husband took a good-humoured revenge by exclaiming in French, with a sly look at me, " See what comes of travelling with ladies!" Reading was such a necessity to him that unable to find time in the day, and having accounts to settle late every night, he would yet when all was done, take up some hard, dry book and compel his tired eyes and languid mind to do a little more work *by way of recreation!* My repeated remonstrances were cut short with "I cannot live without reading." But never did his love of study interfere with his visits or his meetings, or with any branch of his varied work.

He was a diligent and ready writer ; quotations, thoughts, outlines of sermons, things new and old out of his full treasury, were neatly inscribed in note-books and kept for reference. With all his deep spirituality he had a strong vein of humour, which made him get some fun out of almost everything. His stories were irresistibly amusing, and I know of nothing more comic than his " History of the Buggles Family," in which, with a few strokes of his pen and a few graphic phrases, he has immortalized (for us) some of the incidents of our private life. Very interesting and clever also are the descriptions in rhyme of his most important journeys, written to interest those at home. Indeed, wherever he went, whatever he did, he never forgot his " beloved home," his " little Paradise," his " Bethany," as he loved to call it. He did this extra writing in spare moments here and there, when most people would have done nothing. His mind was so untiringly active that rest to him only meant change of occupation.

He left very few subjects untouched, but the one that he sounded to the extent of his powers was how to use every faculty to the glory of God in the good of man.

He was an enthusiastic traveller, and an ardent admirer of fine architecture. His greatest rest and refreshing was to visit some splendid old cathedral and point out all its beauties in detail. He had a little money when he was young, and spent it all on a visit to the Holy Land, of which he wrote a description in his "Recollections of Other Lands." Rev. Canon Whelpton, one of his travelling companions, writes of him :—" He was the mind and soul of the party; he planned, arranged, managed, and directed at every point of the tour; he was always ready with psalms and hymns and spiritual songs to cheer our hearts, to make us enter into the deep meanings of Holy Scripture as illustrated by the scenes around ; above all to invite us by his example, instantly and at all times, to lift up our voices in prayer, that we might reap the best blessings from the high privilege of our pilgrimage."

Some years later one of his aunts left him £200, which he laid out wholly on a journey to America, though it also served him another useful purpose, for ever afterwards any very extravagant act of generosity would be justified by "But 'tis my aunt's money," till the phrase became a joke in the family.

That was the only little legacy he ever spent on anything personal. He had others, but they went straight into the work.

"He that dwelleth in love dwelleth in God, and God in him."

"He will beautify the meek with salvation." (Psa. cxlix., 4.)

As some rare perfume in a vase of clay
  Pervades it with a fragrance not its own,
So when Thou dwellest in a mortal soul
  All Heaven's own sweetness seems around it thrown.
Harriett Beecher Stowe.

Servants of God ! or sons
Shall I not call you ? because,
Not as servants, ye knew
You Father's innermost mind—
His, who unwillingly sees
One of His little ones lost—
Yours is the praise, if mankind
Hath not as yet in its march
Fainted, and fallen, and died !
Matthew Arnold.

VI.

All our dear Evangelists loved their Director as a father, because he treated them as his children. He visited them in their homes, helped them in their difficulties, sympathized in their sorrows, took part in all that concerned them, consulted them as to every little change in the work, and last, but not least, was as gracious and as courtly to them as though they had been the most influential men in the Church (and who can say they were not, if personal effort counts for more than money or position in Divine calculations!)

There was a total absence in him of that antiquated clerical spirit, which still largely prevails in French Protestantism. He esteemed his Evangelists very highly in love for their work's sake, and never made them feel that their ecclesiastical status was lower than his own.

In the leaders' and quarterly meetings what an effective method he had of cooling any too hot argument that threatened to blaze up into a dispute! His gentle " Let us pray " has arrested many a hasty word on its way to wound a brother, and breathed back calm into many a ruffled spirit.

The people loved him. The poor men and women at the halls said his face was a sermon to them. When the news of his death reached Paris our Bible-woman wrote from Rue Clairant that the people were crowding up to her room to get details, and all of them with tears streaming down their faces. She added, " See what a holy life can do ! "

Children everywhere loved him. Sometimes when paying a visit, the little ones of the family would fight for a place beside him, and failing that would get as near as possible in front of him, where they might catch his friendly nod and loving smile.

His was one of those sweet natures that take everything kindly and see good in everyone. He seemed, indeed, an incarnation of the 13th of 1st Corinthians—always encouraging, always generous, even lavishly so ; always magnanimous and forgiving, though morbidly sensitive to any unkindness or rudeness. He never closed his eyes at night without, as he used to say, "feeling nothing but love" in his heart for everybody.

Sometimes when detailing in the home circle any little discussion with detractors or opposers (as plentiful in our days as in Nehemiah's) someone would exclaim, " why did you not say this, that, or the other," suggesting something *piquant*. He would answer, " If I had, I should not have been able to sleep quietly to-night," or " If I had, it would have pained them, and I hate giving pain." Blessed one ! the only pain he ever gave us was when he left us to go " up higher ! "

He had learnt the " new commandment," and his whole life was an act of obedience to it. All who know the Rue Roquépine Church in Paris will remember the passage painted in seven languages behind the pulpit, " A new commandment I give unto you, that ye love one another ; as I have loved you that ye also love one another. By this shall all men know that ye are my disciples if ye have love one to another." That little circular nave may stand for my husband's monument. When it was being painted 32 years ago he spent hours superintending the Hebrew panel. If he left it for an instant something went wrong and had to be repainted. He might well take an interest in the commandment which was the key-note to his life.

He had an ideal beauty of character, which drew his family irresistibly towards him. We have often said to each other, with tears of tenderness in our eyes, " Was there ever anything so lovely, so touching as father ? "

But gentle and amiable as he was, he had a quiet dignity of manner which effectually prevented any undue familiarity or liberty-taking. Moreover, he was so firm and strong in his rule that his antagonists called him obstinate ! Being of a remarkable vigorous temperament morally, whenever he had clearly seen any course to be the right one he would take it and persist in it, despite the most powerful opposition. He never contended, unless driven to it, and was a man of very few words ; but all knew that with him to *say* was to *do*.

Strictly orthodox himself, he yet never repelled any who in this free-thinking country could not see eye to eye with him in matters of belief. All who had the Spirit of Christ were his brethren, no matter to what extent their heads might be affected by heterodoxy. After our first arrival in Paris, Mr. Demogeot, Professor of Literature at the Sorbonne, one of the *literati* as well as one of the choicest spirits of France, began to attend regularly at the Rue Roquépine, and soon formed a devoted friendship for my husband. He hardly ever missed a service, and used to love to have quiet talks with him in our little home above the Church. I cannot vouch for his conversion to orthodoxy, but he certainly had the mind of the Master, and was " not far from the Kingdom." My hope is that the French Agnostic and the English Methodist preacher are now together " in the presence of the King."

"Mark the perfect man and behold the upright, for the end of that man is peace." (Psa. xxxvii., 37.)

"Father, I will that they also whom Thou has given me be with me where I am, that they may behold my glory." (John xvii., 24.)

"We are journeying unto the place of which the Lord said, I will give it you." (Numb. x., 29.)

  Take courage to entrust your love
  To Him so named who guards above
   Its ends, and shall fulfil!
  Breaking the narrow prayers that may
  Befit your narrow hearts, away
   In His broad, loving will.
       E. B. Browning.

VII.

Friday, July 13, was our last day *en famille*. We were at St. Malo for the health of one of our children. In the afternoon our second daughter, our youngest son and myself were carried out by the receding tide while bathing and nearly drowned. After trying in vain to save me, the two managed to swim against the current to the shore and procure help in the shape of our prospective son-in-law. My husband, happily, knew nothing of the danger till it was past. The evening was very quiet and solemn. We half-drowned ones shivered over a blazing wood fire; the others gathered round as near as the heat would let them. We all felt we had just been spared the agony of separation, and could neither speak nor think of anything else. We read chapter after chapter of praise and consecration, sang hymns both French and English, and prayed until bed-time. Surely an antepast of our next family meeting in the eternal Home!

At five next morning my husband was up and off to Paris en route for Birmingham. He never saw any of his children again.

On Friday, the 17th August, he joined me at our brother-in-law's, Westbrook Hay, Boxmoor, Herts., and readily agreed to put off the homeward journey till the following Wednesday, saying he should be glad of two days' more work in London. Those two days, during which he received £1, cost us—his life. On Tuesday, the 21st, he returned to Boxmoor utterly exhausted. His last day of wearisome collecting was done. Being a dark night he had lost his way, and only reached the house about ten o'clock, after half an hour's wandering in the park. That was the beginning of the end. It was no longer a question of travelling on the morrow, and we decided to wait until the Friday. But Thursday evening found him still weak and unfit for any fatigue, and we persuaded him to stay for the next boat on the following Monday. Little did we imagine that that was the date ordained for his last long journey from time into eternity!

During the week he suffered much from pain in the left shoulder and from general weakness, but he refused to stay in bed, and kept about as usual. He even took some long drives and enjoyed them. We all felt concerned on his account, and the various members of the family and household, and also the visitors, seemed to vie with one another as to which should show him the greatest kindness and attention. He must have felt unequal to any effort, as there is no entry in his diary, which he had kept all his life through, after Monday the 20th. But he still wrote letters for money to the friends he had missed on those two dreadful days in London. Truly he ceased " at once to work and live."

As we look back upon that last now sacred week, we remember the peculiar heavenliness of his whole bearing, and wonder we did not read the warning in his ethereal face. It was truly the "shining light" " shining more and more unto the perfect day," which " day " was so much nearer than we thought. It was as though the soul had outgrown the body, and was literally bursting through the bars that confined it.

Did God allow our eyes to be holden so that nothing should anticipate the glad surprise He was reserving for "His beloved "?

On Sunday, the 26th, he rose early as usual, and spent perhaps an hour or more in communion with God. Before going down stairs, after our usual prayer together, he read to me Keble's morning hymn. ("The Christian Year" was one of his very favourite books. His last letter to me expresses great delight at having come across the two volumes of Keble's life by Coleridge on an old book-stall, and dwells upon the pleasure he was having in reading them in the train).

I remember now that he was quiet and subdued, though he appeared really better in health. Before going to church I wrote home that he was "almost himself again."

On entering the little Bourne End Church, the clergyman, Mr. Earl, spoke to him and requested him to read the lessons, but he declined on the ground of his voice being still weak. The sermon was beautiful, almost prophetic in its words of comfort : "I know the thoughts that I think towards you, saith the Lord, thoughts of peace and not of evil, to give you an expected end." (Jer. xxix., 11.)

On the way home he began to be much exhausted, and could hardly manage the short hill. On reaching the house he at once fell asleep until luncheon, and also slept again most of the afternoon. My brother-in-law's fears were aroused and he begged him to see his doctor in London the next morning before starting homewards. He, however, so objected to this and so pleaded with me when we were alone not to say any more about it, promising that if needful he would see a doctor in Paris later on, that we ceased to press the matter.

In the afternoon my sister and I were looking out texts to be engraved on our mother's tomb in Norwood in memory of our father, who lies in an Australian grave. My husband took an interest in and approved our choice, little dreaming that before the next Sunday he would be laid to rest with our beloved mother in the same tomb. Towards evening he sat on the verandah enjoying the gorgeous sunset, peering as it were through the

"gates of space, whose key
Love keeps on that side, and on this side death."

At dinner he seemed to revive, and in the evening conducted family prayers with wonderful vigour. We sang from the Mission Hymn Book—

" Now I have found the ground wherein
Sure my soul's anchor may remain." &c.,

and " Sun of my soul, Thou Saviour dear," &c. His beautiful voice sounded out as sweet and clear and loud as ever. He then read the 4th chapter of 2nd Corinthians, commenting freely on several verses, particularly on " cast down, but not forsaken," and " our light affliction," and " the things not seen," concluding with a fervent prayer.

When we retired to rest my sister begged him to let someone help with his packing, but he answered cheerfully, " Oh no, thank you, I shall get it all done in a trice."

I am glad, however, to remember that I did the greater part of it.

As we were finishing it off he said: " I had such a blessed time of prayer here this morning (in his dressing-room), whoever comes after me in this room will get a blessing, *for God was here this morning.*"

Before 6.30 next morning, God had come again to receive him to Himself.

When all was over, remembering his words, I could only bless the Good Master for having thus set his seal of approval on the habit of early prayer, irradiating His faithful servant's last " morning hour " with a foretaste of the glory so soon to be revealed to him!

Behold, I say unto you, Watch,
Let the door be on the latch
In your home.
In the chill before the dawning,
Between the night and morning,
I may come.
                              B. M.

" Enoch walked with God : and he was not ; for God took him." (Gen. v., 24.)

" Absent from the body...present with the Lord.' (II. Cor. v., 8.)

"I will come again and receive you unto myself, that where I am there ye may be also." (John xiv., 3.)

And we must pass the gates
Of Death linked with Him, holding by the hand
Our Brother gone before, before we come
To the perception how our life is joined
    To God's.
                              H. E. H. King.

One little hour, and then the glorious crowning
The golden harp-strings and the victor's palm ;—
One little hour, and then the Alleluia,
Eternity's long deep, thanksgiving psalm !
                              C. P.

" Thou hast made him most blessed for ever : Thou hast made him exceeding glad with Thy countenance." (Psa. xxi., 6.)

VIII.

My husband passed a troubled night. His mind ran as usual on spiritual things. His "waking thoughts" were always "bright with God's praise."

"God gives His angels charge of those who sleep,
But He Himself watches with those who wake."

He was with His restless child every moment of those long hours.

We did not talk much, as I was so anxious for him to sleep, but he repeated hymns and prayed aloud for strength to "get home" next day to his work and to his children. He quoted—

"Tho' waves and storms go o'er my head,
Tho' strength and health and friends be gone,
Tho' joys be withered all and dead,
Tho' every comfort be withdrawn,
On this my steadfast soul relies :
Father, thy mercy never dies."

and regretted that it had been left out of the hymn in the Mission Book. He was surely allowed to draw my attention to it for my sake, for he no longer needed it himself. Once he began the hymn—

"For ever here my rest shall be," &c.

As it seemed rather an effort to him to repeat it, I took it up and went through the four verses. He responded earnestly. When it came to the 4th verse,

"The atonement of Thy blood apply,
Till faith to sight improve,
Till hope in full fruition die,
And all my soul be love,"

we both endorsed the prayer with a solemn *Amen*—our last united act of worship.

It was about then that he clasped my hand tenderly, and said " My most precious wife, how I do love you !" That was our only farewell.

Towards morning, when the oppressive breathing set in, he said "Perhaps we shall have to wait till Wednesday." I think it was about five o'clock when he began to expectorate blood, but I have only a confused memory of that last awful hour. I aroused help and sent for a doctor, unknown to him as during the whole week he had refused to see one, declaring that he only needed rest and quiet. But long before the doctor arrived the Good Physician had healed him for ever, and taken him where there is no more sickness nor death.

He was his own beautiful self to the end. When a kind attendant put a large hot poultice on his chest, he said "Oh, how nice that feels!" and when my sister came into the room he gave her a sweet smile—his last on earth.

Knowing how he hated either being or seeming ill, I said to him as cheerily as I could, "Well, darling, this is evidently a sharp attack of bronchitis, and we must just wait quietly here a few days longer—a good opportunity for acting submission to God's will." He answered in a very decided tone, "Oh yes, it's all right." After this I asked him if he had any pain and he said, "No." I never once suspected anything wrong with the heart, but I knew he was fearfully ill. It may have been ten or fifteen minutes later, suddenly there came a strong convulsive movement. I rushed to him—only to see the mysterious change which we call death pass quickly over the beloved face, leaving it still and calm in the last sleep.

* * * * *

In the dressing-room everything spoke of life : bags and rugs carefully strapped for the homeward journey, the clothes on the chair awaiting their wearer, the Greek Testament open at the chapter he had read at prayers, with the latest letter from one of our daughters placed between its pages, the eye-glass lying just where he had put it off a few hours before—it seemed *impossible* to realise that he had been caught up suddenly out of our midst, borne away for ever above the need of these accessories of mortal life, above the need even of our affection!

We do not realise it yet.

The following fragments of a poem by Edwin Arnold may comfort other mourners as they have comforted us. A freed spirit addresses the friends who are preparing his body for burial :—

"I can see your falling tears,
I can hear your sighs and prayers ;
Yet I smile, and whisper this,—
'*I* am not the thing you kiss ;
Cease your tears, and let it lie,
It was *mine*, it is not *I* !'

Sweet friends ! What the women lave
For its last bed of the grave,
Is a hut which I am quitting,
Is a garment no more fitting,
Is a cage from which, at last,
Like a hawk my soul hath passed.

. . . . .

Loving friends ! Be wise and dry
Straightway every weeping eye ;—
What ye lift upon the bier
Is not worth a wistful tear.
'Tis an empty sea-shell—one
Out of which the pearl is gone ;
The shell is broken, it lies there ;
The pearl, the all, the soul is here.

. . . . .

God all glorious ! God all good !
Now Thy world is understood,
Now the long, long wonder ends !
Yet ye weep, my erring friends,
While the man whom ye call dead,
In unspoken bliss instead,
Lives and loves you ! Lost 'tis true
By such light as shines for you ;
But in the light ye cannot see
Of unfulfilled felicity,—
In enlarging paradise,
Lives a life that never dies !
Farewell, friends ; yet not farewell ;
Where I am, ye too shall dwell.
I am gone before your face
A moment's time, a little space ;
When ye come where I have stepped,
Ye will wonder why ye wept.

Ye will know, by wise love taught,
That here is all, and there is naught.
Weep awhile, if ye are fain,—
Sunshine still must follow rain ;
Only not at death,—for death,
Now I know, is that first breath
Which our souls draw when we enter
Life, which is of all life centre."

"I know him that he will command his children and his household after him." (Gen. xviii., 19.)

"Let your light so shine before men that they may see your good works and glorify your Father which is in Heaven." (Matt. v., 16.)

"Before his translation he had this testimony that he pleased God." (Heb. xi., 5.)

"As for me, I will behold thy face in righteousness: I shall be satisfied when I awake, with thy likeness." (Psa. xvii., 15.)

"So oft the doing of God's will
Our foolish wills undoeth!
And yet what idle dream breaks ill
Which morning light subdueth!
And who would murmur and misdoubt,
When God's great sunrise finds him out."
       E. B. Browning.

"O Lord my God, do Thou Thy holy will—
   I will lie still—
I will not stir, lest I forsake thine arm,
   And break the charm,
Which lulls me, clinging to my Father's breast
   In perfect rest."
       Keble.

IX.

One of our children says : From our earliest childhood, I say it with reverence, we were able to understand something of the lovingkindness of our " Father which is in Heaven " by the lovingkindness of our father who was upon the earth. The indefinite was made definite to us by specialisation.

Far back as our memory can travel, our father was all tenderness and strength. The boys were sometimes punished, the girls were allowed to grow like flowers, for father had Ruskin's ideas about theirbringing up.

It was a treat when he came up to the nursery ! I can still see him on all-fours, hidden under a great bearskin, pursuing us round the room while we screamed with delight. When we were old enough to sit at the breakfast-table and father had anything which we were not expected to ask for, he would always insist on giving a taste of the coveted morsel to each one of us, unheeding how little might be left for himself !

We not rarely showed a quarrelsome or uncharitable spirit at meals ; in such a case the quiet remark from father that he wanted us to tell him all about William the Conqueror was more of a rebuke than the sternest scolding. It was the same in regard to coming down early to prayers. He did not need to say, " You must come ;" when eight o'clock struck, if we were not down, we would hear a pathetic duet, father's clear voice, and the maids' thin piping, chiming out the hymn, and would be filled with remorse, knowing how he loved to have us all round him before beginning prayers. The change in our outward conduct was thus worked from within, a slower perhaps, but a surer method.

How generous he was ! Eagerly on his return from a journey would we gather around him awaiting the words : " Open your hands and shut your eyes " or " He who loves his home brings back stick or stone !" As we grew older, we loved him for himself. He was a companion and friend, as well as a father. Moreover, we revered his character. We saw how he gave up everything to duty. We knew his strongly developed intellectuality. Yet self-sacrifice was constantly taking the place of self-culture. We knew he felt things keenly, yet we never saw a shadow of irritation cross his face. We knew he was often terribly tired when he went to bed, and yet he was up generally the first in the family for his hour of prayer, "seeking God before the sun." The influence of those morning talks with God pervaded his life. In God's law did he meditate day and night, and he was "like a tree planted by the rivers of water that bringeth forth his fruit in due season."

His whole being was steeped in charity ; if he spoke to us of Christian perfection we could believe in it because we lived with him ! We loved his little courteous ways. I remember our visits to the Rue Roquepine bureau. In the midst of work or shopping we would oftentimes turn in. However busy father was, he would be radiant at seeing us, would get chairs for us with a loving : " Sit-down, sweetests; tell me all you've been doing," etc., etc. No event in our lives was insignificant to him. We knew that nothing that touched us could fail to touch him.

His one earthly ambition for his children was that they should be learned. He used to say laughingly that his dream was to see his girls in white gowns walking up and down the lawn reading Plato in the original !—(a dream never realised !)

He loved Christ with a deep personal love. He loved the cause of Christ, and gave to it all the untiring energy of his whole nature. "Il faut du courage, toujours du courage !" Those words of Napoleon in another kind of fight were the watchwords of his life. Difficulties only stirred his zeal. Out of seeming defeat he organised victory.

The Saturday before his death the Evangelists of the Mission were discussing their chief. "Mr. Gibson never commands us to do certain things" they said, "but he does them himself, and something compels us to do as he does.

He has never told us to be in time for the Saturday leaders' meeting and prayer-meeting, but he is always the first there. We know he is busier than we are, and we are ashamed to be late."

The world saw his energy, his strength, his firmness; we saw that—and his sweetness. Most beautiful was our father to those most near to him. The best things in God's handiwork are most lovely on nearest view.

"The Gospel of Christ translated into flesh and blood" was the universal testimony with regard to him—a living epistle, "known and read of all men."

He dearly loved music. If ever mother and he were at home together in the evening, which was very seldom, and we wanted to lure him down from his incessant writing, mother had only to strike up some music. The charm worked invariably ! A few moments after father would appear beaming with pleasure and quoting "Orpheus with his lute," or "Music hath charms to soothe the savage breast !"

He was full of fun. If ever in family discussions, mother advised a less pacific course than that to which he was inclined, he would smile mischievously and turn to us saying " whom Jezebel his wife stirred up !"

I cannot speak of his devotion to mother, shewn in such countless little ways. He never allowed anyone else to meet her at the train when she returned late from meetings. All those trifling attentions—which are supposed to belong almost exclusively to the period of courtship—he continued them to the end. His entry into the house brought nothing but light and pleasure. We have looked into his bright eyes, always young, and thought of those words of Abelard, " I am sprung from a land of light, the temper of whose inhabitants is light." Surely our father came thence, and now he has returned to the sunny heights of God whence he came.

He had always liked the idea of being taken away in the midst of his work. When he heard of Mr. Barratt's death in Germany he said, " that is the way I should wish to die."

The sunset of his last Sunday evening was a wonder of beauty. How fair a type of the life of him who watched it, his face aglow with worship. In the August of his lifetime, no leaf sere, no leaf fallen, every faculty strong to the last, his own sun was to set upon this earth : a lovely and glorious sunset after a cloudless day !

" Till in the ocean of Thy love
We lose ourselves in heaven above "
were the last words he ever sang.

We see him no more with us, but we do not say *he has gone*; we only say he has gone beyond the limit of our earthly vision, has dropped below our horizon into the ocean of eternity.

And in the midst of our blinding grief we yet lift our hearts in thankfulness to our Heavenly Father, who spared him to remain in our very midst, in sacred familiar intercourse, so long after he was perfected and made meet for the companionship of the saints in light.

We pray for faith that, as our darling read on his last night upon the earth, we may "look not at the things which are seen, but at the things which are not seen: for the things which are seen are temporal, but the things which are not seen are eternal."

"None of these things move me, neither count I my life dear unto myself, so that I might finish my course with joy, and the ministry, which I have received of the Lord Jesus, to testify the gospel of the grace of God." (Acts xx. 24).

"What things were gain to me those I counted loss for Christ. Yea, doubtless, and I count all things but loss for the excellency of the knowledge of Christ Jesus, my Lord." (Phil. iii. 7, 8).

> "O strong soul, by what shore
> Tarriest thou now? For that force
> Surely has not been left vain!
> Somewhere, surely, afar,
> In the sounding labour-house vast
> Of being, is practised that strength
> Zealous, beneficent, firm!"
>
> *Matthew Arnold.*

X.

The Rev. J. Gaskin, of Boulogne-sur-Mer, an old and tried friend, allows me to print the following comprehensive sketch, which he read from his pulpit on the Sunday after the funeral.

"Wm. Gibson was a minister's son, one of the many who have belonged to this Apostolic succession, and have piously chosen the ministry their fathers have adorned. He was first an assistant master at one of our Connexional schools, then President's Assistant and Classical Tutor at Richmond, and afterwards a popular preacher in one of the best London circuits. I well remember hearing between thirty and forty years ago, on the other side of the world, a running description of the leading London preachers by one who was considered a judge. He placed Mr. Gibson in the front rank for clear, vivid, striking, and forceful portraiture, and as a master of pure, nervous, telling English, very ready, never at a loss, always putting his case with clearness and confidence.

Mr. Gibson was a *scholar*, a graduate of London, he gained high distinction, being one of the few who obtained honours in Biblical languages, Hebrew and Greek. He kept up, as many do not, his early literary tastes and acquirements.

Busy as his life was, he seemed to find time for everything, verifying the old adage—that if you want a favour or service ask it of a busy man. I remember seeing him on a cold winter's morning, sitting round the fire with his children, hearing them repeat their lines from "Horace and Virgil," scanning and construing with them as if he had never been anything but a school teacher. He also kept himself abreast with theological and general literature.

Mr. Gibson was a *traveller*, the greatest I have personally known; full of zest and enthusiasm. He knew every point of interest in the places he had visited, seemed instinctively to fix upon all that was worth seeing and remembering, and make it his own once for all. He had visited every capital in Europe, and almost every important town and city in the United States and Canada. He was a familiar figure in every important circuit in Methodism in Great Britain and Ireland, as he was constantly visiting, preaching, and holding meetings for the benefit of his beloved work in France. Paris he knew as well as, if not better than London.

All the English preaching places, as well as the stations for Evangelical Mission Work are of his founding. He built the beautiful little sanctuaries at Chantilly, Aniéres and St. Cloud, and he was constantly looking out for opportunities for starting work in new centres. He would wait and watch for years, patiently promenading the whole quarter, till he found some place for a salle. So he got to know Paris and Paris people as few Englishmen know them.

·But it was as a *Christian*, and especially as a Christian *Minister*, that he made his personality most impressively felt. Mr. Gibson was a very godly man; so godly, that everything else seemed to pale before his complete and all absorbing devotion. He truly counted all things loss for the excellency of the knowledge of Christ. He was consumed by the true Missionary spirit, a quenchless enthusiasm that took account of no obstacles, and scorned all discouragement. His faith was mighty, and ever looked for the removal of mountains in the work to which he had devoted all with loving self-sacrifice. With how Christly a tenderness and compassion he regarded the very lowest and most hopeless of the people for whom he prayed and worked! How nobly he gave up all his prospects of honour, advancement and distinction in the ministry at home, to work in France; and to return, after an interval, to give his life to that work among the most degraded of the population. I know of no more striking instance of a man of refined temperament, choice gifts and wide cultivation, pressing into the service of the lowest and most needy the highest gifts of mind and heart. France has been favoured by Providence with two remarkable men, who have devoted themselves to this mission of loving evangelism—McAll and Gibson. McAll's work has had a wider range, arising out of its founder's neutral position, which excited no rivalries outside of the churches, but drew sympathy and help from them all. Mr. Gibson was the servant of a church, he laid on the altar gifts, which, while they did not command equal apparent success, represented an amount of self-sacrifice and devotion which had no parallel. If Mr. Gibson had had the free hand and free lance of an unattached evangelist, with adequate resources, he would have covered France with an organisation that would have been the wonder of the churches. So complete and all absorbing was his enthusiam, that many of his own ministerial brethren thought him, well, just a little too exclusively pushing and zealous for France. He had France on the brain! How he begged and worked, travelling night and day, crossing the ocean, and from city to city on the American Continent urging the claims of France! France catholic, and France unbelieving, yet France foremost in power for good or evil, demanding the efforts of all Protestant Christendom to make her the brightest jewel in the Redeemer's crown. It would surprise most of us if we could know how many miles he has travelled; how many letters he has written, and how many speeches he has made in his wonderful propaganda. He always secured, by some means, a special meeting at Conference on behalf of French work. Sometimes, as at Birmingham, it was a garden party, sometimes a drawing room meeting, sometimes a more public gathering, but France was always to the front. The wonder is how he got through all the work he accomplished. Many men would have found it impossible to do what he did in the Evangelistic work alone. But besides this, he had all the duties of the Chairmanship, the supervision of all the Stations and District business, and many other secular matters requiring constant attention (besides the collecting of from £1,000 to £1,200 per annum), yet he was a most punctual and copious correspondent. Everything went to his work—heart and soul and body were in it. Often I have seen him after a busy day, not closing till midnight, after which a brotherly talk would carry us to the small morning hours, yet he would be stirring again at six, and punctually at eight, his clear ringing voice would be heard, whoever was present or absent, singing the hymn which began family worship.

Time would fail, and words too, to touch and describe even the salient features of this untiring worker for God. He was just as diligent in works of mercy as in efforts for the conversion of sinners.

I will only add, Mr. Gibson was a man of *prayer*; eminently a man of importunate supplication. Prayer was the foundation of all his work; wherever he went, whether to the houses of friends, or on visits among the people, he never omitted this ; and it was by prayer he ever sought to hearten and keep alive the fidelity and zeal of the agents employed in the work. Often he would invite them to his house at St. Cloud for an all-day meeting of prayer. To many, such a mode of spending a day would seem a weariness to the flesh ; not so to our saintly friend. His face seemed to brighten, and his spirits to rise as the hours rolled by. When evening and parting came he seemed like a giant refreshed with new wine.

Mr. Gibson was a remarkable combination of firmness and gentleness. Once convinced a course was right, nothing could make him swerve. Some thought him in consequence gently obstinate; but it was only his high sense of moral rectitude which was in play. He could not do what his conscience did not fully approve ; expediency was not his law ; he would have made a perfect martyr in persecuting days. Yet he was the essence of sweet kindliness. His smile won the love of innocent childen. One of mine was very much attached to him, and asked once why he liked him so much, said " Why, because he has the goodest face." Gentle he was and gentlemanly, full of the quiet meekness of Christ.

The end came suddenly and unexpectedly. After forty-two years of unceasing toil, he ceased at once to work and live. None was ever more ready for the final summons. I never saw him more full of life and energy than shortly before; yet such labour as his must tell on a man when he has passed the three score.

The anxieties of the last few years had also probably something to do with the conditions which ended in the sudden and unforeseen break down. No evidence of this was apparent in the calm and unruffled bearing of Mr. Gibson, either in his official or private life, but deep down beneath the outward calm there must have been troubles and anxieties, fears for the ultimate success and prosperity of his loved work, which would prey on his sensitive nature.

But now the rest has come, with its fuller light and perfect vision. The wise Master builder has said "It is enough, enter thou into the joy of thy Lord." Our dearly loved and honoured friend rests from his labours, and his works do follow him."

"He was a faithful man and feared God above many." (Neh. vii., 2.)

"An Isrealite indeed in whom is no guile." (John i., 47.)

"And in their mouth was found no guile, for they are without fault before the throne of God." (Rev. xiv., 4.)

And when we come to die we shall not find
The day has been too long for any of us
To have fulfilled the perfect law of Christ.
H. E. H. King.

"If I still hold closely to Him
What hath He at last?
Sorrow vanquished, labour ended,
Jordan past!"

XI.

Subjoined are some extracts from a few out of many magazines and journals which contained notices of my husband's death with short outlines of his life. I have selected only what I hope may tend to set his beautiful character in still stronger relief and to exhibit him as an example imitable by all, since the Source whence he drew his strength is open to all.

The Rev. H. F. Bland, now of Canada, writes to the *Christian Guardian* (Toronto) :—

In 1841-42 the Rev. Ralph Gibson (William's father) was stationed in the Addington Circuit. A most excellent man he was, transparent and earnest. The future French Missionary was then, say ten or eleven years of age, slender, pale, and thoughtful. As a missionary collector my recollection of him is very fresh—persistent, not to be said nay. How that thin pale face and silvery voice would plead! The successful pleader of other days was in that boy-collector. Circumstances for many years threw us widely apart, but I followed Mr. Gibson's subsequent steps with deep interest . . . . Seldom have I been more impressed than when I read of my brother's sudden death. " The law of truth was in his mouth, and iniquity was not found in his lips : he walked with God in peace and equity and did turn many away from iniquity."

In the *Methodist Recorder* of Aug. 30 Rev. N. Curnock says : There was great consternation in the Mission House on Monday when the news arrived that the Rev. William Gibson, B.A., of Paris, had suddenly passed away. . . . . . At the Birmingham Conference, Mr. Gibson appeared to be in his usual health. We dined with him at Mr. Akrill's in company with Dr. Jenkins and Rev. E.

Workman. He was full of enthusiasm about the work to which he had devoted so many years of his life, and was preparing for the great Garden Party in Mr. Akrill's grounds, at which the claims of the work were to be advocated. Those who were present will long remember the thrilling stories he told during dinner of his adventures in Paris during the Commune, and of the extraordinary Providences which surrounded our Methodist people throughout that time of fiery trial. Last Wednesday we spent some time with Mr. Gibson, arranging with him the details of an article on that subject, which he had promised to write for our Winter Number. He was then working under high pressure for his mission. His intention was to return to Paris in a few days, and he very much wished that we would accompany him, not for pleasure but for work—always " work—Paris—France. What will you do for France?"

The Rev. D. A. de Mouilpied lays " a flower upon his grave " in the following letter to the Methodist papers :

The mournful and unexpected intelligence of the death of my former colleague and dear brother reached me so late that it was not possible for me to be present at Norwood at the laying of the mortal remains of my dear friend in their last resting-place. May I ask of your courtesy to be allowed to lay a flower upon his grave? The death of Mr. Gibson is a great loss to the Church of God on earth. He was the soul of goodness. His kindness never failed. His geniality was a constant inspiration and cheer. His hopefulness was unbounded. " The gospel of the face " was always preached by looks and smiles which were flashed from an inner light which always burnt steady and clear. He was the best of friends ; his kindness never wearied, it was never exhausted. He was good to all, but his friendship was a very generous friendship. His activity was the revelation of his consecration to his work, and that was complete. The fire burnt with inextinguishable blaze on the altar of his soul. Although a most modest and gentle man, purpose in him was very strong ; and, once a course of action had been entered upon, nothing could turn him aside. But so transparent was his motive, so genial the way in which he enforced his will, so quiet his method, that what in some might be called self-will, and in others obstinacy, was in him the virtue of perseverance. It is hard to think that we shall see his face no more till the Resurrection Day. His has been a life well-spent, and now he rests from his labours.

In "Work and Workers" for October Revs. Dr. Rigg and F. W. Macdonald bear testimony to the life, the labours, and the character of their old friend :

We have never known a saintlier or more absolutely consecrated soul than William Gibson. A holy passion, an unquenchable enthusiasm burned with a clear and unremitting light on the altar of his heart. For thirty years he had given himself, body and soul, to evangelistic work in France. He was working for the same object to the very last. How for so many years he had unrestingly, and with unabated zeal and fervour, kept up his work of faith and labour of love at a high pressure level, seldom reached, even at intervals, by ordinary workers, had been a marvel to all who knew him. At length he sank exhausted in the race, the energies of his physical nature having finally collapsed. The wonder is that the speed and pressure were so long maintained. His working days were longer

by hours than those of most men, even busy and active
men ; his cares and anxieties were urgent and excessive.
Fervour and faith had sustained him, and would have sustained him still, but that the overwrought and exhausted
body yielded at length, and gave way. All who knew
Gibson and his work, all who cared for the great cause of
evangelistic mission work in France, will deeply mourn the
loss of such a worker, the quenching of such a light, the
passing from view of an example so apostolic ; but no
one who knew him and his work can be surprised at
the result.

Mr. Gibson was the son of a Methodist minister. He
was converted at Woodhouse Grove School in 1848. From
that school he passed forward to Wesley College, where he
took an active part in religious work, maintaining the
warmth and fervour of his zeal throughout his period at
the school. He entered the ministry in 1852, and in 1854
was assistant to the Rev. John Farrar, the President of the
Conference. He was appointed to Paris for his first term
of residence in 1862, having previously spent five years in
London circuits. After ten years' work in Paris, he
returned to the English work, and spent six more years in
London in the Southwark and Brixton Hill Circuits. In
1878 he returned to Paris, and there he spent the remainder
of his life with an ever-increasing devotion to his work, to
which he had given himself with an absolute surrender.
The paramount importance of France as a centre of worldwide influence was perhaps his deepest intellectual conviction ; the need of the Gospel for France in order to heal
its national troubles and maladies, and to make it the most
powerful and central influence in the world for the
leavening of humanity with the Christian truth and

Christian faith, were ideas which had taken possession of his whole soul, and the force of which only increased with the increase of his knowledge and experience. He was further convinced by the evidence of large and wide experience that whilst Christianity as represented in the worship of the Calvinistic Reformed Churches was unsuitable to the genius of France, the bright, vivid, sympathetic, experimental characteristics of Wesleyan Methodist doctrine and fellowship were peculiarly adapted to win the sympathy and allegiance of the French people, adapted to their temper, their tastes, and their whole spirit. He appreciated fully the difficulty of inducing Frenchmen, impregnated with the ideas of Calvinistic Presbyterianism, to accept Protestantism in the emotional and experimental forms of Wesleyan Methodism, but he held that one reason why Protestantism in France has produced an almost inappreciable effect upon the nation was the unsuitableness of the old form under which it had been known for centuries. What he sought to initiate was the presentation of Methodism in its special and characteristic aspects to French people—its presentation in the generous freedom of its Gospel doctrines, and in the hearty and social forms of its Christian fellowship. Although in his work he stood as a leader well-nigh alone in Paris, and had but a very small handful of fellow-labourers in other parts of France, his experience and the measure of success granted to him, were sufficient to warrant the conclusions which he had fixed in his own mind, and which he cherished for the encouragement of his fellow-labourers and himself in their work.

The work accomplished by himself and his family in the preparation and publication of hymns suitable for French

Methodist worship, and tune-books, and tracts, and
evangelistic periodicals, has formed no mean part of
what has been done in the pioneer services of Methodism
in France. It may be safely affirmed that those who enter
into the labours of Mr. Gibson and his circle of associates,
will discover more and more, as their experience expands,
how great a work of preparation has been accomplished.
The evangelistic spirit and services of Methodism, its
prayer meetings, its fellowship meetings, the frank, cordial,
and loving relations it establishes between the members of
the Church, its true brotherhood and sisterhood, have
taken hold of the working people of France in a number of
important centres.

Never was a pioneer placed in more difficult circumstances than Mr. Gibson. Never did a labourer for Christ
do work of exceeding difficulty in a nobler spirit, with
higher faith, or in a more exact and whole-hearted correspondence to the spirit and the precedents of Apostolic
Christianity. What the world needs is that its waste
places, where Christ and His saving truth are still unknown, could be occupied everywhere by evangelists of the
spirit and character and aims of William Gibson.

J. H. RIGG.

My acquaintance with Mr. Gibson began when he was
stationed in the Chelsea circuit more than thirty years
ago. I was but a boy at the time, and was from the first
impressed by his amiability and gentleness. He took a
kindly interest in my welfare, and was one of the first to
encourage me to tread the path which, in Methodism,
leads to the ministry. He has often referred to my first
public address, delivered at a Sunday School meeting at

Westminster, early in the year 1860, and would quote the undeserved but kindly prophecies he made at the time. During the early years of my ministry, I visited him more than once in Paris, where the passion for what was to be his life work had already taken possession of him. From that time onward I enjoyed his friendship, and he took the place in my esteem and affection which he retained to the end. With increasing intimacy I had a continually deepening admiration for his purity, his unworldliness, his absolute devotion to God and His work. During the last three years our intercourse has been close and constant, and I have had the best means of gauging the intensity of his love for the special work committed to him. The way in which his thoughts and aspirations, his endeavours and his prayers converged upon "the Gospel for France" was wonderful, at times pathetic. With him all roads led—to Paris. In a far truer and deeper sense than that in which the English queen said, "You will find Calais written upon my heart" might it be said that France was graven upon the heart of William Gibson. He lived and died for it. How he laboured for it many know in part; none but his own family know the whole. Along with a gentleness that nothing could ruffle, a patience that nothing could exhaust, he had courage, perseverance, and tenacity of purpose that I have seldom, if ever, known equalled. They carried him through innumerable difficulties, they secured for him again and again the ends upon which his mind was set, and turned the seemingly impossible into accomplished fact. Though he was characterically, I had almost said, incurably sanguine, yet I can well believe that the work in which he would never admit the possibility of failure cost him more than others thought, more than he himself knew. The sudden, the unlooked for failure of his vital powers would seem to show that he had been spending them all along in a way he little suspected, so unaccustomed was he to consider himself, or take account of days spent in toil and nights in travel.

When it was first proposed, a year or two ago, to place the Evangelistic work he had so long directed upon a new basis, drawing it into closer association with the French Conference, the proposal was not altogether welcome to him. This was natural. Humanly speaking, it was his work; he had made it. Its every detail was planned and administered by himself, aided by his admirable family, and he was not to be blamed if he thought that no one else would love it, care for it, toil for it as he delighted to do. But he came to see that it was better that responsibility should be shared, and that a future must be thought of when he could no longer do for his beloved work what he had done. No trace of self, no pride of authority or precedence mingled with the hesitation he felt with regard to certain portions of the scheme proposed, and he set himself to promote the desired reorganisation, placing all his varied resources at the disposal of the Committee with the utmost loyalty and good will.

How little did we think that his work was already done, and that others must face the problems of the future unaided by his counsel and his prayers.

Dear William Gibson! He has left a memory that will long be cherished by all who knew and loved him, cherished by the poor people for whom he lived as their friend and father, one whose wealth of love and sympathy had given them their first notions of the love of God, whose Christlike life even more than his earnest words had drawn them toward the Kingdom of Heaven. F. W. MACDONALD.

At the meeting of the General Missionary Committee, Rev. F. W. Macdonald referred to the recent sudden death of the Rev. William Gibson—"William Gibson, of Paris," said he, "for he has been associated with that field of work in a manner more close than is usual. Very few men are bound to a particular sphere of interest so closely and by so many ties as Mr. Gibson has been for the last twenty-five years. The Committee is aware how pathetically sudden was his removal. It is only two months ago that I was with him at the French Conference at Nimes. I playfully said to him, 'You are never ill, and you are never tired.' 'No,' said he, 'I don't think I am very much—I have very much to be thankful for'—and he at once set off on a fifteen hours' journey. We all saw him at the Conference. His spirit was as bright, gentle, gracious, and earnest as it always was. There had been no period of rest or preparation, but few men have lived in such a state of preparedness for the Master's call as Mr. Gibson, and perhaps when the immediate shock and distress shall in some measure have passed away, even those nearest to him may see the gentleness and beauty of God's dealing with him—a man who was allowed to live in his work to the very last, putting into it his heart's devotion and mind's intelligence, and then without any cares or gathering up of tangled issues suddenly called away to his reward. He has left a lovely memory, as we all know. Many of us have had occasion to differ from Mr. Gibson in matters of detail—but how small do such differences appear when we look back upon the career that has just closed. He lived a spotless life, and he has left behind a blameless memory."

Dr. Jenkins said: I feel that this event is to myself a profound personal loss. I knew Mr. Gibson in the intimacy of a spiritual fellowship for many years. We wanted more of that kind of work which he was well fitted to render to a society like this. But we wanted even more, a longer career of an example which I will venture to say connot be exceeded (if matched) for the singular completeness of its consecration. I always counted it an honour to have fellowship with Mr. Gibson in the work of God and in addressing the throne of grace together as we have often done, and I do not remember in any friendship that I have formed a higher sanctity of inner life expressed, as many of us know, with beautiful consistency. He was not a Frenchman, and yet he was; and France never had a more faithful and zealous friend than Mr. Gibson; and he has left a record in Paris and in France that time will not soon efface.

Dr. Rigg said he had known Mr. Gibson for many years. A purer or a saintlier man never lived. He thought he never knew a man so absolutely consistent with his own modest—(never vaunted or loudly expressed)—but living example and character of consecration to God.

Rev. G. W. Olver, B.A., said that for during a period of ten years he had to correspond with Mr. Gibson on all sorts of questions relating to his own work and workers in connection with the French Conference, and he never knew him utter a single angry word. He could well understand what was said to him (Mr. Olver) by one of the members of the family on the day of the funeral: "Tell them that he was Christ-like in his family. We never knew him raise his voice in anger. We never saw him with a frown upon his brow."

Rev. John Bond writes: I remember my dear friend in his earliest ministry. We came out the same year, and were appointed to adjoining circuits in South Wales, he to the extensive colliery and manufacturing circuit of Merthyr Tydvil, and I to the small agricultural circuit of Brecon. We first met about 16 miles from our respective homes. He was then in the youth what he was known to be in later life, good nature embodied. We were friends in an instant. It was impossible that it should be otherwise, so hearty was his greeting, and so transparent his character. Overflowing with fun, crammed with curious tales of his habitual and rough environment, inexhaustible in stories of considerable European travel, with a large heart full of sympathy for the good wherever found, and a cultivated mind competent to judge justly of what he saw, he was the most pleasant companion possible. In the exuberance of our young manhood we roamed the fields and jumped the ditches of the wild Wales of those times, like two boys let loose, and time fled all too rapidly. We probably never afterwards met, even for a few minutes, without joking over our first intercourse, when he had a horse to drive which he declared could not go, and which I declare he did not know how to make go. But behind this genial fun no one could fail to see the sanctified spirit, and the broad outlook and sober purpose of a noble Christian minister. His work then and there won for him esteem and admiration. I never met him but he did me good.

Mr. E. R. Shaw, who was my husband's fellow traveller in America in 1878, kindly writes as follows:—

This American tour was undertaken by Mr. Gibson in the interval between the close of his superintendency of the Brixton Hill Circuit and his entering on the duties of the post to which he had recently been appointed by the Conference, viz., that of General Superintendent of our Methodist Evangelistic Work in France.

France, indeed, as a Mission field had been Mr. Gibson's early love, and he had already laboured successfully for several years in that country. It can hardly be doubted that one motive which strongly influenced him in making this tour was the opportunity it would afford him of awakening among the educated classes on the other side of the Atlantic a deeper interest in the Mission to which, as it has proved, he was destined to devote the remainder of his life. A large majority of those who come to visit Europe from Canada and the States make a more or less extended stay in Paris; and it is interesting to note that of late years an ever increasing number of these have found their way to our Wesleyan services in the Rue Roquépine.

Mr. Gibson was in every way an excellent companion for such a tour as this. He had already travelled much; his spirits were buoyant; his observation was keen and rapid; his interest in the novel and ever varying incidents which each successive day presented was intense; while as a companion he was cheerful, kindly, and genial in a rare degree.

But it was easy to see that, underlying the strong feeling of enjoyment, rising at times to enthusiasm, which grand natural scenery never failed to awaken in him, there was ever present to his mind a profound sense of the sacredness of his life-work, and especially of that work in connexion with the spiritual needs of France. France seemed to be ever in his mind; France was often on his lips; and it needed but some chance word, or some subtle association, to divert his thoughts from the most impressive natural surroundings, and fix them on the great work which lay before him. "It is France," he said to me more than once, referring to Queen Mary's exclamation when she heard of the loss of Calais, "It is *France* which will be found engraven on *my* heart."

Mention has already been made of the geniality and general charm of Mr. Gibson's companionship. None indeed who met him only occasionally and for brief intercourse could fail to be struck with the exceeding winsomeness of his manner, and the unaffected kindness of heart which literally shone from his countenance. But a period of three months' close association can hardly fail to disclose traits which casual intercourse would scarcely reveal. Each successive week which we spent together served but to deepen the impression which I had already formed as to the transparent simplicity, the guilelessness, the single-mindedness of his character, and of that real saintliness of life which is the result alone of entire consecration. Here was the secret of so much that was lovely, so much that was truly noble.

In conclusion, it may be confidently said, that, when the history of Methodist pioneer missionary work in France shall be written, one of the brightest names on its pages will be that of the Rev. William Gibson.

"I know that my Redeemer liveth." (Job xix., 25.)

"God will redeem my soul from the power of the grave : for He shall receive me." (Psa. xlix., 15.)

"I will ransom them from the power of the grave ; I will redeem them from death. O death, I will be thy plagues : O grave, I will be thy destruction." (Hosea xiii., 14.)

"When this corruption shall have put on incorruption and this mortal shall have put on immortality then shall be brought to pass the saying that is written : Death is swallowed up in victory." (I. Cor. xv., 54.)

> The grave is the dark keyhole of our life
>   That holds within it locked the mystery
> Wherewith our days are rife.
>   But we alack ! have lost the key ;
> And now we can but peep and pry
> At the beyond, or bow our ear
> Some far-off harmony to hear,
>
>   *   *   *   *   *
>
> Waiting till He who hath the keys come near.
>   *Ellice Hopkins.*

> When from the dust of death I rise
>   To claim my mansion in the skies,
> Even then this shall be all my plea
>   Jesus hath lived, hath died for me.

XII.

This account of the last sad service is taken from the *Recorder* of Sept. 6 :—

The mortal remains of "William Gibson, of Paris," were laid to rest in what may almost be termed the Methodist plot of the vast and beautiful south-east London cemetery on Friday last.

*   *   *   *   *   *

The service in the cemetery chapel was read with great solemnity and feeling by Rev. F. W. Macdonald.

An address followed by Rev. G. W. Olver, B.A. He said : We have not forgone the words of Christian comfort with which we are accustomed to gather round the Christian's grave. There was not one of them which we could not take to ourselves. We do not come here merely to bury our dead, nor do we come to praise a brother who has passed out of sight. But I have been asked to say a word or two regarding him. Yet I confess I have never undertaken a duty which I have felt a greater strain upon mind and heart. I have said that we have not come here to praise, but I wish in a few words to recall the gift which God bestowed, and which He has now treasured in His safe treasury till our turn shall come, and we shall join the company of those who rest. All who have learned from the Scripture the true character of life, of its privileges and its responsibilities, know that whatever talents are possessed by men are the gifts of grace. Ability for service is not to the living an occasion for pride. To him who receives it, and to those who watch its use it is matter for thanksgiving, and especially to him who receives it is it matter of responsibility. The Church has seldom had a worker more unselfish, more devoted to the work laid upon him, than William Gibson. From a youth he loved the

Saviour. He found peace, I am told, at the age of eleven, while singing the Doxology. My own first knowledge of him goes back forty-five years. We met casually, but from that time I have known him, and of late years his service also. We first met when we were both visiting London to pass an examination. For the last thirteen years we have worked in close intimacy. Those who knew him in public knew much of his work; those who knew him privately knew much more. Quiet, gentle, beloved—because so loveable—if he had a fault it was that his unselfishness and devotion to the welfare of those among whom he lived led him to what might be thought an excess of generosity. If that were a failing, at all events it leaned to virtue's side. To his work he gave himself, his wife, his children, and that united band has built up a work which some present who have come from France know full well. The place vacated by William Gibson God only can fill. His service was not showy, but quiet and persevering. Nothing satisfied him but the conversion of souls. To that work he gave himself with a persistence which was wonderful, and with a success which will be his abundant joy when the Master shall come. After all, whatever of sombreness or sadness there may be around us to-day, that coffin shows that God has once more fulfilled His latest promise. Day by day we look for the fulfilment of many of his promises. His last was, "I will come again and receive you unto Myself, that where I am there ye may be also." If there be sadness and sorrow in our hearts to-day, yet we have confidence that our Father and Friend will fulfil every promise as it is needful for us, till He fulfils the latest and last, when He gathers us in his arms and takes us to His peace. Perhaps He may fulfil it to us as He did to him. On Sunday night he conducted family worship with simplicity and fervour, and a manifest experience of the truth he spoke. He dwelt upon the words "Our light afflictions, which are but for a moment, shall work out for us a more exceeding and eternal weight of glory, while we look not at the things which are seen, but at the things which are not seen ; for the things which are seen are temporal, but the things which are not seen are eternal." Then he retired to rest. He had a troubled night. At 5.30 came a sudden attack of the heart : in another hour a sudden convulsion, and then all was peace. May God write those words respecting "our light afflictions" upon our hearts! Only, if we want the comfort of them, we must look " at the things which are not seen." Our brother is out of sight, but not out of reach. We cannot talk with him, but we have fellowship with him in Christ. He is among "the cloud of witnesses." It is not for us to say whether he may not be among those "ministering spirits sent forth to minister for them who shall be heirs of salvation." He and we walk with Christ : and in Christ day by day we have true companionship. He remembers the things of earth—he must do, if the song is "to Him that loved us, and washed us from our sins in His own blood." Let us see to it that with simple trust we give ourselves to fulfil the Master's task till the Master calls. One thing more. We can pray that God will, in his own way, provide for the consolidation and carrying on of the work to which he gave practically all his ministerial life. With deep emotion, which for a time quite checked his utterance, Mr. Olver added, As to those on whom the shadow most deeply rests I cannot trust myself to speak ; but we know that the Father will compass them with the arms of His loving mercy, and hush the weary spirits to His own perfect peace.

A favourite hymn of Mr. Gibson's, repeated by him during the Sunday night, was then sung heartily and with evident feeling by the congregation, beginning—

" For ever here my rest shall be
Close to Thy bleeding side."

Mr. Olver then closed the service in the chapel with a touching and appropriate prayer.

The closing services at the graveside were read by Rev. G. W. Olver, who, just before the conclusion, mentioned that Rev. George Whelpton wished to say a few words on behalf of the bereaved churches in France.

Mr. Whelpton, who had difficulty in controlling his emotions, said he had been asked to represent the French churches and to express their deep affection for one who had been more than a father to them, who were dearer to him than any outside his own family. Some there could understand the affection which existed between a missionary and his converts. On the previous Tuesday, when the sad news came, the weeknight service at Rue Clairaut was turned into a testimony meeting, and the hall re-echoed with sobs. Yet they were full of praise to God for all he had accomplished by His servant. He was to have brought a palm branch bound with the tricolor, as an emblem of the victory of their departed brother. This had been subscribed for by all the members of the Paris Circuit, but had not yet arrived in London. All the members of the various halls had also sent addresses of condolence. Mr. Gibson's people in France said of him that his home was their home, and that he was the dearest, and his smile to them the sweetest thing upon the earth. The one characteristic in him above all others was his exceptional holiness of character. All recognised his blamelessness of heart, his singleness of intention. He never lost an opportunity of praying with his colleagues, and bringing them to the footstool of Divine mercy. During the last fourteen years Mr. Gibson had been to him (Mr. Whelpton) as a father. One present there from France had said to him that morning that Mr. Gibson's life had been a living Gospel. His choice of hymns, especially on the subject of entire sanctification, was very beautiful. It was not only his own people who loved him. Outsiders did the same—even unbelievers. A gentleman—a stranger—saw him one morning carrying two travelling bags to the St. Cloud Station, and insisted upon relieving him of one. On hearing of Mr. Gibson's death, this man said, "I am an outsider, but I heard him say some words which I shall never forget." The faith which inspired such a life must be not only sincere, but faith in a reality. To him (Mr. Whelpton) the message from that open grave was to seek holiness of heart. Above all things, William Gibson lived with God. They praised the Heavenly Father for His gift, and in saying *au revoir* to their departed brother looked forward to their next and happier meeting.

The Doxology was then sung, the Benediction pronounced, and the gathering slowly dispersed.

*   *   *   *   *   *

We terminate this fragmentary sketch with the following beautiful extract from the leader in the *Recorder* of Sept. 6, 1894 :—

" New and pathetic reasons for united intercession come to us constantly. William Gibson, with ' France ' written on his heart, has died praying. We rise from the writing of these lines to go to his burying, and as we go there comes to us the sorrowful persuasion that only a comparative few in the Methodist Church had any conception of the deep and passionate yearning which possessed him with reference to the evangelisation of France. With a haunting fear that some well-meaning but terribly ignorant persons in Methodism are resolving to agitate for withdrawal from the whole Continent of Europe he has passed into that world where they see all things in unclouded light. Let any intelligent Methodist, who has time and means at his disposal, make a journey to France and inquire into the possibilities and necessities of the work for which William Gibson was begging and praying when he died. He will come again asking, Who can fill this empty place? *And why, during his lifetime, did we not all more earnestly support these outworks of Protestantism in France?*"

* * * * * *

Oh may God raise up many to more than fill the "empty place"! William Gibson's prayer will not be fully answered till *Christ* has seen of the travail of his soul *in France* and is SATISFIED.

HELEN W. GIBSON.

St. Cloud,
France.

END.

PARIS DURING THE COMMUNE, 1871:

BEING

LETTERS FROM PARIS AND ITS NEIGHBOURHOOD.

WRITTEN CHIEFLY DURING THE TIME OF

THE SECOND SIEGE,

BY

WILLIAM GIBSON, B.A.

(*Republished after his death for the benefit of the French Methodist Mission.*)

TO MY WIFE,

MY CONSTANT COMPANION DURING THESE DAYS

OF TROUBLE, THIS BOOK

IS DEDICATED.

PREFACE.

I HAVE been frequently asked to give an account of what I saw in and near Paris during the time of the Commune. My easiest answer is to reprint my letters written in March, April, May, and June, which have already appeared in some of the public papers.

4, Rue Roquépine, Paris,
Nov. 11th, 1871.

Paris after the Siege.

4, Rue Roquépine, Paris,
March 6, 1871.

As soon as I have a moment at leisure I fulfil my promise to give you an account of my journey to Paris. On reaching Boulogne I was not even asked to show my passport, I suppose because I was so unmistakably English. Not finding a train to go on at once to Paris, I stayed at the Hotel Christol, and left Boulogne the next morning at nine o'clock. The train was quite full, for the most part of people returning to their homes in Paris. As soon as we had fairly started, I looked about me to see who were my companions, and found a Frenchman and his wife returning to their home at Colombes, near Paris, a comical old French lady, a German who had lived in England many years, and spoke English perfectly, a shrewd Scotchman, an Austrian from Vienna, and a Prussian *(pur sang)* who could speak French pretty well, and English badly. The Frenchman and his wife had lived at their house at Colombes all through the siege; he had been in the National Guard, had been in the midst of the fighting at Avron, and had taken part in the sortie of the 19th January, but had been in no special danger, his post being at Bezons, some little distance from the actual fighting. His bodily appearance did not indicate that he had suffered much, for he was fat and flourishing, but his wife looked as if she had known what it was to be put upon short rations. This quondam National Guard asserted that the world was making a retrogade movement, that the reign of brute force was returning, and that, in the point of view of civilization, the results of the war were most disastrous. All the nations of Europe would increase their armaments, and the time would be long deferred when Europe would become a community of nations in which international quarrels would be settled by arbitration and not by the sword. The queer old French dame declared that if the Hohenzollern pretext had not come up, Bismarck would have found some other excuse for going to war. All agreed in thinking the terms too hard, and that it was only a long armistice, not a peace. The German with an English look and an English tongue expressed a very strong opinion against the hardness of the terms, and so did the Scotchman. The Austrian said that the ex-Emperor, knowing the hatred against Prussia which existed in the South German side, hoped to have enlisted them on his side; but the South German States knew that if they sided with France their territory would have been the seat of war, and their land would have been laid waste and their towns destroyed, and they were not anxious for that; and besides, they remembered the days of Napoleon I., and therefore had decided to fight with Prussia against France. The Prussian *(pur sang)* maintained a judicious silence on all political questions, and only talked when general topics were discussed. He was on his way back to Paris, where he had been for some years in business. He knew his path would not be made easier in Paris by declaring himself a German, so intended to keep silence and not uselessly declare his nationality. There was nothing different from ordinary times in the railway journey as far as Noyelles, where we first caught sight of the spiked helmets, and were made to feel that the line from this point was in the possession of the Germans. At Abbeville there were numbers of German soldiers. Indeed, there are three thousand quartered in the town. The black and white (Prussian) flag was suspended in the middle of the station, and all betokened a thorough German occupation. The querulous old lady interjected, "*Cela me fait mal*," declared that the Germans were savages, true Visigoths, and like all those people of the North. She made, however, the *amende honorable* soon afterwards, for she added that she understood they had behaved very well at Abbeville. At Amiens the buffet was not open, and it was a poor look-out for those who had not been thoughtful enough to bring provisions with them. A few eatables were sold at the buvette, but they were terribly dear. Our thrifty Scotchman had to pay 2f. 50c. for a skinny leg of fowl, a piece of bread, and half-a-bottle of vin ordinaire. The station was filled with Prussian soldiers; and the platform was made the scene of much excitement by the fact of some travellers being turned out of the train to make room for some German soldiers. Our ladies expressed themselves more strongly about this than all the other miseries and humiliations of the war. At last we were at Creil, and found the station hung with garlands and Prussian flags, and almost covered with evergreens to celebrate the victory of the Germans! Leaving Creil (one of the places on the Paris Circuit plan), we found we were going not by Chantilly, but on the Pontoise line, and soon saw the reason in the broken railway bridge over the Oise. Nearing Pontoise, we saw many proofs of the devastations caused by war in gutted or pillaged houses. At Pontoise we were informed by a railway official that we must all get out of the carriages, that we should have to walk along the temporary bridge over the Oise, and should find a train awaiting us at the other side of the river. So we quickly descended, took our portmanteau or carpet bag in hand, and walked on the planks over the river, the water rolling close under our feet. 'Twas a sight to be remembered, that procession across the Oise. On the other side I got into a carriage with two Prussian officers, fine-looking men, who sat mute for some time, but at last drew out their beautifully-executed maps of the environs of Paris, and asked in broken French where Ermont, the station at which we were now stopping, was to be found on their maps. We were soon at St. Denis, where the Prussian officers quitted the train. The St. Denis station was literally crowded with Prussian soldiers. Passing the town, we had a good opportunity of witnessing the havoc made by the bombardment: houses roofless, or the roofs broken in several places; a great factory gutted, the new Catholic church much injured, and a scaffolding at the side of the tower of the cathedral for repairs to the fine old pile, where all the old kings of France used to lie, each in his own house. Passing the desolate *zone* and the fortifications, we were soon at the Gare du Nord. But instead of finding the asphalted area full of cabs, as before the siege, there were only three or four cabs and three omnibuses, and they were all engaged. Outside the station, however, I was fortunate enough to find a *voiture de remise*, which soon conveyed me to Rue Roquépine.

I am thankful to say none of our chapels have been in the least injured during the siege. Even Asnières, which has been under the fire of Mont Valérien, and half-way between the German battery at Argenteuil and the North of Paris, has not been damaged externally. Yesterday, being so few, we met in the minister's house. Five were present, two of them strangers from London. The three who have been in Paris throughout the siege, were full of expressions of thankfulness to God for his care over them. They were all well, and had been so throughout the whole time, though at times weak through want of sufficient nourishment. One cause of thankfulness was that they had the provisions which I had laid in for the siege, without which they would have been reduced to great straits.

I have this day taken a general view of some of the principal parts of Paris, and find them less changed than I anticipated. The trees both in the Boulevards and the Champs Elysées are much as they were. Very few have been cut down. The gardens of the Tuileries are artillery barracks; the statue representing Strasburg is covered with flags and garlands, as it was before the siege, but they are dirty and faded. It is also covered with faded immortelles. Each statue in the Place de la Concorde had a black covering over the face, that they might not appear to look on the Prussians when they were in the city last week. In the Rue de Rivoli, the Rue Royale, and Boulevards, the one great change is the want of carriages, cabs, &c., in the streets. In the Rue St. Honoré at one o'clock I could not see, looking down from the corner of the Rue Royale, a single wheeled vehicle. The Mobiles are beginning to leave Paris. I was aroused at five o'clock this morning by the *rappel*. What was it? Not, I am thankful to say, the usual call to revolution, but simply a call to the Mobiles to get ready to start, an announcement which would give great joy to the inhabitants of this quarter on whom they have been billeted.

4, Rue Roquépine, Paris,
March 7, 1871.

I cannot find words to express the gratitude of our people here for the provisions sent from the Mission-house, as soon as the way to Paris was open, which arrived most opportunely. *The services in this chapel have never been interrupted*, and on two or three special occasions the chapel was crowded. I have this day been to Asnières. The chapel itself has not been injured in the least. The depredations committed in the interior—the forcing open of doors, the injury done to the harmonium, the wrenching off the box for contributions at the door, and other acts of wanton mischief, are what might have been anticipated. As I left the train numbers of German soldiers were mounting to go on to Versailles, generally choosing the upper portion of the carriages, to get, I suppose, a better view. To go to Asnières you must now take the Versailles train, not, as formerly, the St. Germain line. No trains as yet are advertised to go to St. Germain, and only five trains in the day to Versailles, instead of, as before, every hour. The trains consist almost exclusively of second class carriages, the first class having doubtless been appropriated to the use of "*ces Messieurs*," the term by which some Frenchmen, whether in anger or otherwise it is hard to tell, invariably speak of the Prussians. I walked through the village of Asnières, making my way along the Rue St. Denis, and returning by the Quai de Seine on the banks of the river. But few of the inhabitants of Asnières have returned to their houses. There are many signs of both French and German occupation—broken windows, palings and hedges partly destroyed, dilapidated gardens. German names were here and there chalked on the walls of the houses. I entered one house which had been the peaceful and happy abode of our Asnières chapel steward before the siege, and found it the home of filth, the precious legacy of the Mobiles. The Germans have nearly all quitted Asnières to-day. One good man with a "Red" cap, after diligently sweeping out his house, was making a bonfire in the street of the débris left by "*ces Messieurs*." On nearing the bridge, or rather what *was* the Asnières bridge, I saw the broken piers projecting from the water, the rest, except the remnants of some of the arches, being all destroyed. Pity that the French should themselves have committed so much useless injury to their own property! In Paris the word "Ambulance" still meets you in every direction. Private houses by scores and several hotels still display the flag with the red cross. Part of the Western Railway Station is also still so employed. I find more dogs than I expected, and fancy that dog's-flesh eating, like the Irishman's fast horse, existed more in imagination that reality. True, the poor brutes, like too many poor human creatures, look dreadfully thin, but their number seems to me not much diminished by the siege. Although there is now gas in the streets, it is as yet but a flicker compared with the brilliant lighting of Paris as it used to be. Coals are still scarce and dear. Our coal merchant, as a special favour, got us some two days ago, and was obliged to charge eighty francs per ton. Provisions are now plentiful and cheap, but people have no money to buy, all industry having been so long at a stand-still. The labouring men are weak, and unequal to hard bodily toil. The coalmen, who used to think nothing of shouldering a sack of coals, now shrink from carrying a load to the third or fourth story. Caricatures of the ex-Emperor meet you in nearly every shop window, and caricatures of the Emperor of Germany, and Bismarck also abound. The general talk is —all these disasters are owing to the Emperor Napoleon. Some of the National Guard, without venturing to fix any blame on him, say that twenty years was quite long enough to reign, and now they wanted something else! This Paris is a wonderfully buoyant place. Everything is returning to its normal condition. This " return of peace " is like the return of spring after a hard winter.

March 8, Evening.

I have had a most interesting day. Went to the Chemin de Fer de l'Ouest to go by an early train to Versailles. When I asked for a ticket for Versailles I was asked if I had a special " *laissez passer;*" and, as I had not, could be booked no further than Viroflay. My compartment was quite full, and in a short time I heard no little vituperation vented against the Prussians. One woman next to me came from a village three miles beyond Versailles. They had Prussians quartered upon them at the beginning of the siege, and they had been there ever since, never having been engaged in fighting, but in "eating, drinking, and drilling." As we passed along we saw many houses almost entirely destroyed. At Viroflay I set off to walk to Versailles. At last I came to the great gates at the entrance of the town. A great number of people were assembled outside the gate, but no one was allowed to enter without a "*laissez passer.*" Some German soldiers formed the guard to see that no one entered to whom permission had not been given, and a little man in Prussian uniform who could speak French was examining the papers. As the crowd were beginning to push him, the little official screamed out for two of the Landwehr. My passport, which had fortunately been *visé* by the Prussian Consul in London, got me easily through, and I began at my leisure to walk along the Grand Avenue leading towards the Palace. Now a few spiked helmets passed, now a German officer on horseback, and now, as I neared the centre of the town, twenty or thirty iron boats for making pontoon bridges, placed keel upwards, each drawn by six horses, crossed the road, probably beginning their journey back to Germany. I had now before me the front of the Palace, and there was floating over the centre of the Palace of the *Grand Monarque* the Prussian flag! Under the shade of this emblem of foreign dominion were the statues of the celebrated French generals, and the equestrian statue of Louis XIV. In the restaurant of the Hotel de France, I met several Prussian officers, some of them evidently of high rank. In the open space in front of the palace were arranged great numbers of field guns. On the walls of the houses were announcements printed in French and German. I passed into the gardens. Groups of Prussians were scattered here and there admiring the beauty of the place. From Versailles I took train to St. Cloud. The houses at St. Cloud are nearly all destroyed. Some beautiful villas which I have often observed with admiration, but the interior of which I never hoped to see, are completely gutted. I made my way to Montretout to see the German redoubt, and to witness the scene of the struggle during the sortie of January 19. Ascending the hill I came to places where the road had been barricaded with earthworks, surmounted by strong boughs of trees—German outposts these to prevent the advance of the French to the redoubt. At last I was in the centre of the redoubt. Wonderfully strong earthworks, deep trenches, and rough stonework covered with iron bars, surmounted by thick layers of earth to protect the artillerymen, are the chief features of the place. From Montretout you gain a good view of Valérien. Descending I had a good opportunity of seeing German soldiers at drill. It was wonderful to see the simultaneous agility with which they instantaneously obeyed the word of command.

Returning to St. Cloud, I passed through the Rue d'Orleans, a terrible scene of devastation, and at last made my way to the Palace. It is a complete wreck, most piteous to behold—only the bare wall standing. I walked through those once magnificent apartments, now an utter ruin. Frenchmen were everywhere loud in execrating the Prussians, though Valérien is accountable for nearly all the damage done at St. Cloud. As I returned to Paris I had three Prussian officers in the compartment with me, and I got into conversation with them. I told one of them I thought they had demanded too much indemnity. His reply was, " The expenses of war."

We had a delightful service at the Rue Roquépine this evening. There were not many present, not more than seven, and we had the class meeting afterwards. From the funds placed at my disposal to help the sufferers in Paris, I was able to relieve one poor woman who is in the greatest poverty and distress as the result of the siege, and whose stepson died yesterday in the hospital. She will thus be enabled to give him a decent burial. Many blessings are invoked on English people for their generous charity in this crisis of need. There is still much misery, and I venture to make an appeal to British Christians for additional help for the relief of their brethren in Paris and throughout France.

I hear on every hand of sufferings endured through the siege, and invariably as among the very severest sufferings I hear enumerated the having to form *queue* at four o'clock in the winter mornings and wait at the doors of the butchers' shops till ten or eleven o'clock for the small ration of meat. Some of the shops are beginning to get gas, and I suppose soon we shall have it again in the private houses.

Thursday, March 9.

This morning I had a visit from a contractor *(entrepreneur de maçonnerie)*, an honest, respectable Frenchman, who has a real *home* in Paris, with twelve children about him, and his opinion was that the misfortunes to France were to be traced to these four causes—1. Want of religious faith. 2. Want of respect for authority. 3. Want of a spirit to *work*. 4. Want of modesty, shown in a spirit of boastfulness and vainglory. For himself he felt that France had been unfortunate, but he did not feel humiliated. They had been pursuing their peaceable occupations, and had been all at once, without any wish on their part, plunged into war. What they wanted now was to set to work, and to be content to work, and things would right themselves.

I have spent a portion of to-day in pastoral visitation. The two or three members of my flock now in Paris live at great distances from each other, and each one had much to say. All were thankful for their portion of the provisions, which, being distributed on Jan. 31, were worth at that time more than gold. All had attended our French Methodist services at the Rue Roquépine. Their faith had never failed, even at the darkest times of the siege, and the way in which their wants had been supplied had sometimes seemed to them almost miraculous. When the cannon first sounded they were inclined to tremble, but gradually they became accustomed to it, until at last they were uneasy if they did not hear it, for the great noise, and the shaking of windows, &c., was from the forts, and when it ceased they feared something dreadful was going to happen. In my walks I passed the Parc Monceaux. The gates were kept by the National Guards, and inside the principal entrance were rows of French cannon. Beyond the second railing were French soldiers with their tents, &c. It afforded me great pleasure to find that none of the noble trees of the Park had been cut down. Some of the smaller ones may have disappeared, but they can be easily replaced. I made my way also to the Jardin des Plantes, and expected to find it comparatively a desert. What was my surprise, then, to find all the animals in their places just as before the siege. There was the huge elephant pushing out his great trunk beyond the bars of his enclosure, the lubberly hippopotamus lying flat on the ground, the scaly rhinoceros opening wide his mouth as usual, to receive contributions of bread or other eatables; the lions, panthers, tigers, &c., all pacing their dens, and looking as sleek as if nothing extraordinary had been transpiring. I suppose I must now believe that all the animals one read of as being killed and eaten were from the "Jardin d'Acclimatation," and not from the Jardin des Plantes. In the principal streets to-day were vast assemblages of the Moblots, who are just about to leave Paris to return to their homes. Several of the streets in Paris are losing their old names—for example, Rue de Berlin is to be Rue Richard Wallace, to perpetuate the memory of the munificent charity of our countryman; and the Rue d'Allemagne is to be Rue de la Revanche! Everybody says the peace is but a truce. "*Ce n'est qu'une trêve,*" you hear on every hand. Nearly all the ladies are dressed in half mourning. How can the daughters of France be merry when their country is in sorrow? The general opinion of Parisians is that the German entry into Paris was a foolish thing, and that it only deepened the resentment of France. If the reason is given that it was important to let Paris know she was beaten, the reply is that the sober people knew too well that France was under the foot of the conqueror, and that nothing will convince the mob of Belleville. Some are of opinion that Prussia will have reason to regret the 1st of March, 1871. Various placards are to be seen on the walls. One at the Mairie, Batignolles, exhorted to contribute towards a general subscription so as to raise the amount of the indemnity at once, and thus get rid of the invader. Another, headed "*Ligue Anti-Prussienne,*" strongly advised all employers of labour to refuse any application made by a German belonging to the States that have made war with France, and in case any Prussian should re-open his house of business, that no Frenchman should ever cross its threshold. In their present temper Parisians cannot be made to understand that this is a suicidal policy.

Paris is now assuming its former brilliant appearance at night. In side streets the dim petroleum lamps may still be seen, but in all the principal thoroughfares the gas supply is the same as it was before the beginning of the siege.

CIVIL WAR IN PARIS.

4, Rue Roquépine, March 10, 1871.

I managed to secure a *voiture* this morning, and drove to Belleville. All was quiet. I then made my way to Montmartre, to the very top of the hill. Some of the " Reds " of the National Guard have taken possession of this elevated ground, and have cannons and other munitions of war. I could not gain admission. The National Guard at the entrance had orders to let no one pass. He said, however, that he would call the corporal, which he did, but the corporal could not let me pass without an order from a superior officer. Through the doorway, however, I saw piles of shells ready to be launched upon Paris, if the occasion should arise. The ostensible reason of the fortifying of this height was to oppose the entry of the Prussians, but now, notwithstanding the central Republican authority, these " Reds " hold Montmartre. Most people say that rather than make them conspicuous by opposing them the Government mean to let this thing die out by its own intrinsic weakness and folly. My cabman was a true Parisian. "We were sold, we were not beaten!" "On Sunday week there was great agitation all along the district from Belleville to Montmartre. The Prussians heard of it, and dare not come in, as they intended, on Monday!" At the extremity of one of the streets at Montmartre I saw the remnants of a barricade, the large paving stones all torn up, and all made ready to form in a short time an impassable barrier. In the exterior Boulevards all the way from Belleville to Batignolles were long lines of sheds for the lodging of those Mobiles who were not billeted on the houses. But they are all preparing to quit Paris shortly, and these sheds will soon be taken down. By the circular railway I have also to-day been all round Paris, starting at the Avenue de Clichy and going round by Charonne, Rapée Bercy, and Point du Jour to the Gare St. Lazare. The line for the greater part of the distance (twenty miles) follows the fortifications. I had a good view of the works constructed during the siege. Wherever there was a wall near the fortifications it was pierced with loopholes through which to fire upon the enemy. As we neared Point du Jour I saw some of the effects of the bombardment. The roof of one large building had been smashed in two or three places. I scarcely recognised Auteuil, with nearly all the trees of the Bois cut down. Placards are posted at the Mairies, exhorting the people of Paris to betake themselves to their ordinary work.

March 11.

A day at St. Denis. I was anxious to see what had become of our preaching-place at St. Denis, so I made my way thither by the 11.25 train. There are only five trains in a day now to St. Denis, instead of one every hour, as before the siege. As I came out of the station I found that a regiment of Prussian soldiers was marching through the town. I walked alongside as far as the Cathedral, and from the steps had a good view of the soldiers as they marched along. First came the artillery, then the infantry, next the ambulance waggons and men with the red cross on the right arm; then the cavalry, then another company of men with the red cross and ambulance waggons. Just what one has read is their order of battle is their order of march. It was very exciting to see the whole street as far as the eye could reach bristling with bayonets, to hear the German martial music and the soldiers singing "Die Wacht am Rhein." As soon as the regiment had passed I took at my leisure a careful survey of the exterior of the Cathedral, to see what damage had been done. Part of the beautiful parapet on the north side has disappeared, several bits of the exquisite stonework of the fine old building and a portion of the roof of one of the towers have been destroyed. I tried to gain access to the interior of the Cathedral, but the *German* sentries would not let me pass. So I went to the German head-quarters in the Rue de la Boulangerie and got a pass to enter. Very little damage has been done to the interior, possibly because the walls were covered with sandbags. One bomb entered and carried away a corner of one of the monuments. Otherwise no damage has been done. I wandered about as I listed, without *gardien*, in this wonderful edifice, and saw more of the tombs of the kings than I had ever seen before. From the Cathedral I hastened to see our little place of worship in the factory now belonging to Thompson Frères, but formerly leased by Mr. Isaac Holden. As I neared the place I found everywhere marks of terrible destruction. Scarcely a single house which had not received one or two bombs. Some were completely riddled. At last I came near the Double Couronne and turned to the right along the route de Gonesse and was soon in our old preaching place. What was my sorrow to find that the walls were shattered, the roof riddled, and the floor partly ploughed up. Three shells had burst in the room where for five or six years we have held services since the present occupants have been in possession, and where for eleven years, while Mr. Holden was tenant, Methodist services were regularly held. An old attendant at the services made his appearance and took me over the factory. The walls were pierced in all directions, rafters carried away and beams broken. In one of the apartments adjoining the factory, formerly occupied by Mr. Holden's family, a woman was killed on the spot, while in the act of dressing, by the very first shell that was sent into St. Denis. In one part of the factory I saw a pile of shells two feet high, all of which had been found within the building. From the upper windows of the factory I distinctly saw Le Bourget, where so many skirmishes occurred. I went next to to the Protestant establishment in the Avenue Benoit, consisting of chapel, day-schools, and pastor's house. The school escaped injury ; but M. Saglier, the pastor, told me that one shell had fallen in his house and three in the chapel, completely destroying the left-hand gallery. In returning to the station I looked into the new Catholic Church, and counted thirteen holes in the roof. It is said that it was struck by no fewer than fifty bombs. Prussian soldiers were to be seen all over the town of St. Denis, making the people feel that they were conquered, and yet generally conducting themselves well.

4, Rue Roquépine, Paris,

March 17, 1871.

A few days ago I visited the battle-field of Champigny. We formed a party of five, and started early in the morning, so as to have the day before us. One of our number was Mr. Scheffter, the young French minister who remained in Paris throughout the siege, had witnessed from a distance the battle of Champigny, and after the battle had helped to carry away the Prussian and French wounded. We made our way along the line of the Boulevards to the Bastille. The red flag was floating from the top of the column of July, and the lower portion of the column was decorated with tricolour flags and immortelles. Having some time to wait for a train on the Vincennes Railway, we strolled into the Faubourg St. Antoine, partly to show the strangers in our party the scene of former revolutions, and partly to see if all was now quiet in the chosen home of the *ouvriers*. All is peaceful enough now, but who will say what may soon transpire? With the emblem of "Red" Republicanism floating over our heads in antagonism to the powers that be, we may well be said to be living on the side of a volcano.

By the rail we soon reached Joinville. On our way from the station to the bridge over the Marne we passed some German soldiers packing their knapsacks and getting all in readiness for their march homewards. They were from the duchy of Baden, and had been stationed at a post three miles further from Paris, the Wurtembergers having occupied Joinville. They were "heartily tired of the war, and were anxious to get home." We had now arrived at the temporary bridge, the entrance of which was guarded by a little Bavarian, who contrasted both in stature and bearing with the fine and portly Prussians whom we had seen north of Paris. Walking on the main road from Joinville to Champigny, towards the crest of the hill where the battle had raged most fiercely, we saw the first sign of a recent fight, shortly after leaving the Marne, in the skeleton of a horse left to bleach in the sun. Mr. Scheffter told us he had seen several horses completely demolished in an incredibly short space of time. The soldiers surrounded the fallen horses, and, after flaying them, each cut a piece from the carcass to supply his own need, and so in a few minutes the bones were left clean. Some carcasses were taken back to Paris to increase the supply of horse-flesh in the city.

As we passed on evidences of a severe struggle were plentiful enough. Not a house that had not been almost demolished, not a wall unpierced with holes for musketry fire. We could generally distinguish the houses and gardens which had been held by the French from those held by the Germans, the hole made by the French being generally round, that by the Germans a mere slit in the wall broadening outwards. We now reached the village of Champigny, a mere mass of ruins. One poor woman just returning to her house was gazing with mingled grief and despair on the wreck of her former dwelling, and told us that she and her husband had put their all into the building of this house, and now they were left homeless and without resources. A strong barricade, now broken through the middle, had been thrown across the street of Champigny. On each side of this barricade were carts piled with beds, bedding, chairs, tables, &c., the household effects of families returning to their homes. Turning from this street to the left, we were soon, under the guidance of Mr. Sheffter, upon the actual battle-field. " Along this path I and another carried a wounded Prussian officer. He was so heavy that we almost fainted under the load. As we bore him along on the litter he said, ' *Cela ne vaut pas la peine.*' (It is not worth the trouble.) Having placed him in the ambulance, we returned to the field. It was now dark, but, stumbling over the stiffened corpses, we could hear, in a tone weak and tremulous, ' *blessé* ' (wounded). We succeeded in picking up thirty or forty French soldiers who had been wounded at break of day, and had been lying on the cold damp ground all day without anyone coming near to bind up their wounds." [It will be remembered that this battle of Champigny was on the occasion of the famous sortie made by Ducrot on the 30th November to 2nd December, when he led out his troops to the war-cry, " Dead or victorious."] Advancing along the rising ground, we came to a house completely riddled with shot and shell. The proprietor, who was hard at work putting it into repair, had been in the engagement, and gave us some particulars as to the principal points of the combat. We were soon at one of the Prussian batteries, left just as it was when the Prussians were here, *minus* the great guns which had dealt such havoc on the environs of the great city which, grand and beautiful, loomed in the distance in front of us. There was Fort Nogent, yonder Rosny, still further to the right the plateau of Avron. When we could withdraw our gaze from these distant objects, we saw that the ground at our feet was strewn with képis, some of them shot through, showing how fierce had been the fight on this very spot. We now pursued our way over wild fields, dotted here and there with clumps of trees, the ground still rising. The whole field was completely covered with the remnants of cartridges, bullets were plentifully strewn on the ground, and here and there were holes in the mould made by the falling and explosion of a shell, in other instances a round hole only betokened that the shell had entered and without exploding had buried itself in the soil. I need not add that we refrained from meddling with the beds these bombs had made for themselves in the earth, lest we should add the necessary percussion and be ourselves blown into the air! Sad indeed was it, as we wandered about, to see the graves of both French and Prussian soldiers. A little enclosure surrounded with stones and containing three crosses attracted us. On one was written, in German, "Here lies ——, died Dec. 2, 1870." A similar inscription on a second cross—a young Prussian officer just twenty years old. On the third cross was an inscription, but a white *foulard* was wrapped around it, as though to say, "Touch me not." Further on we saw on a large cross, "Here lie fifty Frenchmen." Two others with "Here lie twenty-five Frenchmen," "Here lie fifteen Frenchmen." We went to another mound which we saw in the distance. The mould had just been thrown over the body, but not sufficiently to cover the lower part of one limb, or the shoulder, covered with the soldier's coat, of. the left arm. Such the unlettered grave of an uncoffined Prussian soldier. We had seen enough, and returned with saddened hearts to Joinville. On reaching the Place de la Bastille we found it filled with an excited crowd. There had been a fracas in a neighbouring wine-shop, and some National Guards were conducting all the offenders towards the guard-house.

* * * * * * *

March 18.

This day (Saturday) has been a day of great excitement in Paris. Having occasion to go to the Northern Railway Station at six o'clock this morning, I heard the National Guards in all directions beating the *rappel*, and knew something must be brewing. Young Rostan (son of the Alpine missionary) who came over with 300 young Frenchmen from America at the outbreak of the war to fight his country's battles, and was in the middle of the fight at Montretout on Jan. 19, went to Montmartre and found what was the cause of the tumult. The Government having determined on strong measures to quell the insurgents at Montmartre and take away their cannon, there had been a struggle in the streets. Rostan saw one officer of the *gens d' armes* carried away dead, and another officer with his face much battered, and a poor woman shot accidentally in the street carried away dead. All Paris was speedily in a tumult, and has remained so all day. Going along the Boulevards, I saw numbers of National Guards, disarmed troops of the line sauntering along, knots of people at the corners of the streets. I found that the Boulevards omnibuses did not give *correspondance* along any of the omnibus lines in the direction of Montmartre, Belleville, or Menilmontant, which was ominous. Arrived at the Place de la Bastille, I found the whole square lined with troops. Turning into the Faubourg St. Antoine I observed that all the shops were shut. By-and-bye our omnibus driver wheeled round the omnibus, and went back by the same road that he came. One of the large postal omnibuses *(Administration des Postes)* did the same thing. The turn in the street soon revealed the cause. There was a barricade just thrown up, and men were still at work with pickaxes tearing up the paving-stones, and throwing them on the barricade. The foot passengers were returning on the causeway. " *On ne passe pas* " was heard on every hand, so I turned back too. The Boulevards, as I returned, were in a state of the greatest excitement, and so they were this afternoon. They say that the troops of the line are fraternising with the National Guard—*i.e.*, that part of it opposing the Government and determining to keep possession of the cannons. How the thing will end it is difficult to say. Two proclamations of the Government, signed by Thiers and the other members of the Government, have been placarded on the walls of Paris, one early in the morning announcing their determination to put down the disturbances at Montmartre and elsewhere, and exhorting the people to work and quietness: and the second, at three o'clock this afternoon, assuring the Parisians that they were not preparing a *coup d'état !*

9 p.m.—Our quarter is quiet, but National Guards and *gens d'armes* are patrolling, and a line of National Guards is keeping the approaches of the Place Vendôme.

11 p.m.—We hear the roll of cannon, but hope, nevertheless, to sleep in peace.

4, Rue Roquépine, Paris,
March 20, 1871.

Paris could hardly be said to be "agitated" yesterday as it was on Saturday, for all the population in the city, the National Guards included, seemed to be giving themselves up to enjoyment, the people promenading as usual on Sunday, and the National Guards marching along the middle of the streets. Indeed, all had a complete holiday air. Preceding most of the battalions of the National Guards were young women (one to each battalion) dressed in képi and Bloomer costume, with a small cask suspended by a strap flung over the shoulders. The Place Vendôme was filled with the National Guards, who had possession of the *Ministère de Justice et des Cultes*. A barricade of paving-stones, with two box-seats of carriages thrown on the top, prevented access to the square in front of the Hotel de Ville from the Rue de Rivoli. A similar barricade thrown across the Avenue Victoria prevented access in that direction. A great crowd pressed along the Rue de

Rivoli and the Avenue Victoria up to these barricades; but none, except the National Guard, was allowed to pass by the narrow opening in the middle of the barricade, which was most strictly guarded. The square in front of the Hotel de Ville was filled with National Guards, who seemed to have nothing to do but to enjoy themselves in the bright sun. The omnibus traffic was suspended. It was quite a strange sight to look along the whole line of the Boulevard des Capucines and Italiens from the corner of the Madeleine, and, with the exception of one or two cabs, not to see a single wheeled vehicle, and this at half-past four o'clock on Sunday afternoon, when the Boulevards are usually so crowded with omnibuses and carriages of every description. The asphalted causeways, however, were crowded enough. Very blessed was the contrast from the scenes outside presented by our quiet sanctuary. Both the services were better attended than could have been expected.

To-day in our quarter the city presents a quiet appearance, but I am told that at Batignolles there is a good deal of excitement. When I went to the post-office near the Madeleine this morning one of the officials asked, " What do they think of us in your country?" and added, " C'est comique; un nouveau Government chaque jour!" On Saturday the red flag was no longer on the top of the column of July, but it now floats over the great clock in the centre of the Hotel de Ville. The Revolutionary Committee has issued several proclamations. Most of the shops are shut, and business is almost at a standstill. Two generals, Clement Thomas and Lecomte, were shot at Montmartre on Saturday afternoon.

Monday Evening, March 20, 1871.

The barricades are still kept around the Hotel de Ville, and the centre of the Place de l'Hotel de Ville is filled with cannon. The "Central Committee" has, however, issued no more proclamations, but this evening a placard is posted on the walls, signed by Louis Blanc and others, announcing that two points will be considered : (1) the appointment of officers of the National Guard, and (2) the election of the municipal council by all the citizens. Here is a conversation between two women standing on a bench and looking over the barricade into the Place de l'Hotel de Ville. "And those two officers who ordered the soldiers to fire." "Yes, and it served them right, they paid for it with their life." "And that Trochu, who's he? Such villany, to feed us with that wretched straw, and have all the while stores of provisions hidden away."

March 21, 5 p.m.

Paris is much quieter to-day—no marching of troops of the National Guard, as yesterday and the day before, along the principal streets ; most of the shops are open, and the omnibuses are for the most part running as usual. Still there are groups of people talking most earnestly at the corners of the streets, and there is much excitement and but little business. On going to the Hotel de Ville an hour ago we found that the barricade in the Rue de Rivoli was not kept as yesterday; indeed, it can hardly be said to be a barricade at all, for the people were permitted to walk through it in single file in two places. All the soldiers have been withdrawn from the barracks; and even the gardens of the Tuileries, which have been used as artillery and cavalry barracks, are deserted. According to report, the Assembly at Versailles will not deal with the insurrection with a high hand, but will come to terms with the leaders of the National Guard. At present, however, the Hotel de Ville is still held by the National Guard, and cannon are still pointed along the Rue de Rivoli and the Avenue Victoria. The people, both yesterday and to-day, are promenading in the Boulevards and principal streets as though it were a national holiday!

Wednesday, March 22.

To-day was fixed by the "Central Committee" for the elections for the "Commune," but a placard was posted on the walls yesterday signed by the representatives of twenty-seven daily papers, begging the electors to take no notice of the summons to register their votes.

I went to Montmartre before breakfast this morning, but all was quiet. The numerous barricades, as, for example, those at the end of the Rue Blanche and neighbouring streets, were guarded each by a single National Guard. I counted nine cannons in the Place de Clichy. The barricade at the end of Rue d'Amsterdam had been partly demolished, and was left without any guard at all. A strong feeling is setting in throughout the respectable quarters of Paris against the usurpation of the " Reds." The insurgents made a descent on the Mairie of the 7th Arrondissement last evening, and possessed themselves of it. A few wounds were inflicted: one man had his hand thrust through with a bayonet, but no lives were lost. The Mayor announced by placard this morning that, being turned out, he can no longer discharge his functions!

From half-past ten to eleven o'clock this morning there was constant cannonading. Our windows shook, and we wondered what it was all about. On going out to see I found that it was the Prussians still in possession of some of the forts, who were firing blank cartridge in honour of some " Prussian anniversary." At least so informed me a placard in our boulevard, which ran to this effect: " Salvoes will be fired to-day from the Prussian artillery. We hasten to inform the inhabitants of Paris of this fact, the only object being to celebrate a Prussian anniversary." While, however, I was reading this placard a man came up to me and said, " Yes, they say that ; but do you know what the Prussians are doing ? They are making entrenchments between each fort.

Two o'clock.

I hear that fighting is going on in the Place Vendôme. The young man who told me this says that several people were killed close to him.

Evening.

This afternoon, about two o'clock, the "friends of order" made a demonstration along the Rue de la Paix, towards the Place Vendôme. " Vive la Republique," " Vive l'Ordre," were the watchwords. As they drew near the end of the Rue de la Paix, the insurgents who occupy the Place Vendôme fired on them. Several were killed and many wounded. The crowd fled. The news spread like wild-fire through the city, and all Paris was in a ferment. Our Boulevard (Malesherbes), generally so quiet, was filled with anxious faces. Groups gathered here and there to discuss the situation. Well-affected National Guards were marching with quick step and determined look along the asphalted pavement. The general talk was that one and all were resolved that this state of things should not continue, and that the death of the unarmed victims in the Rue de la Paix should be avenged on the insurgents. At five o'clock we walked along the Boulevard des Capucines. The Rue Neuve des Capucines was guarded by insurgents, who allowed no one to pass. The pavements of the Boulevards were crowded; but scarcely any carriages or cabs, and no omnibuses, were to be seen in the carriage way. The end of the Rue de la Paix was blocked with a compact crowd. It was said that cannon and mitrailleuses command the street, and that the houses also are occupied by the insurgents. The Grand Hotel is occupied by the National Guards, who are the " friends of order," and access can only be gained by one of the side doors, which is kept by the National Guards. The idea is to surround the insurgents in the Place Vendôme. We are about to meet in our peaceful week-evening service, but I do not expect many, as it will be dangerous to venture out to-night.

Night.

Eight persons were present at our service, notwithstanding the perils of the streets. At our class-meeting, after the service, two of our members gave thanks to God for their merciful preservation from imminent danger. One of them, a dentist in the Boulevard des Capucines, close to the Rue de la Paix, joined the " friends of order " in their friendly demonstration, and was nearly at the front when they approached the Place Vendôme. Their spokesman said to the insurgents, " We wish to have a Republic, we're all Republicans ; but we want order. *La crosse en l'air!*" Some of those in the front rank did throw up the butt-end of their muskets. But from behind seemed to come an order. The ranks advanced. A roll of the drums and two taps repeated three times, and at the end of the third time a volley was fired along the Rue de la Paix. A man fell dead close beside our young friend. It was five minutes before he could get out of the street, so great was the crowd and confusion. A second volley was fired, and a third, and men, women, and children fell. All were full of rage against the insurgents, Women, with faces distorted, and looking more like fiends than human beings, were brandishing knives and scissors.

Another young man, a member of our class, had been in his office in the Rue Basse du Rempart, and hearing a noise in the Boulevard, rushed out in the direction of the Rue de la Paix, where the crowd seemed to be the thickest. Hearing that firing was going on, he drew back into the Boulevard just in time to avoid the volley. A poor man was wounded very near him, and was carried into a neighbouring house. A few minutes afterwards he went to inquire how the poor fellow was, and found him dead. The report is that thirty or forty were killed or wounded. It is a sad sight to see two ambulance waggons passing along our Boulevard Malesherbes about three o'clock in the afternoon to pick up the wounded in one of the streets of Paris! It seems, however, that the insurgents would not for some time allow the ambulancemen to pick up the wounded, and some who ventured into the Rue de la Paix to succour the wounded were fired upon.

Thursday Morning, March 23.

I went out this morning into the Boulevard des Capucines and to the end of Rue de la Paix. All was quiet compared with the excitement of yesterday. A number of insurgents were keeping guard at the entrance of the Rue de la Paix. Well-disposed National Guards were keeping the Grand Hotel. Nearly all the shops along the line of the Boulevard are shut. National Guards fill the place de la Bourse. The insurgents are threatening to take possession of the Mairie of the Second Arrondissement, the only Mairie not as yet in their power. The National Guards are determined to resist them.

Afternoon.

Paris is perfectly calm this afternoon. No excitement in the streets. The insurgents are left in peaceable possession of the Hotel de Ville, Ministères, and Mairies. This was the day fixed by the Central Committee for the elections, but as very few went to vote, the elections have been put off till Sunday. What the Government at Versailles will do, it is impossible to say. Surely this state of things cannot be suffered to continue.

Evening.

This afternoon, having occasion to pay a visit in the Rue d'Albe, I had to pass for some distance along the Champs Elysees. A lady whom I went to see in the Rue d'Albe gave me a more consecutive account than I have been able to get from anyone of the sufferings endured through the siege. The effect produced on my mind by the recitals of most people with whom I have conversed has been a medley of ideas, without beginning, middle, or end. " I get credit (she said) for being a heroine, but such credit I do not deserve, for the truth is that, invalid as I am, I lacked courage to go away. Once fairly shut in, I took it for granted that it would be an affair of five or six weeks, little imagining that it would be five or six months before Paris would be open again to the world. Having, however, an account at my banker's, I thought I would not trouble myself, as I should be able to secure what money could buy. But what was my dismay when my messenger returned with the reply, ' Communications stopped with England ; cannot cash your paper.' What was to be done ? A lady happened to be with me at the time, and seeing my emergency offered to place at my disposal 1,000 francs, an offer which I gladly accepted. Before this store was exhausted a French gentleman residing near came, and, although not himself overburdened with cash, offered, so far as he was able, to lend me money, and I was thus supplied. At first, although the prices were high, all the necessaries of life were easily procured. But at last the question of meat became a serious one. So long as horseflesh was abundant I managed pretty well, but when that also was rationed, the prospect became very gloomy. I could not bear the idea of living on bread and wine. Of bread I seldom eat much at any time, and such bread as we were then reduced to, being a compound of bran and chopped straw, I had a perfect loathing of ; and of wine I take but little. I remembered, however, to have read years ago, in 'The Last of the Mohicans,' of a method the Indians adopted to preserve their meat, and having managed to secure a filet de cheval, I tried the process with success. I was reduced, however, at last, to a state of sadness and despair. The bombardment was terrible; the windows of my apartment shook, and the house itself trembled, although no shell fell nearer than the Trocadero. During the last three weeks no amount of money availed to procure the necessaries of life, and if the siege had lasted a week longer I must have died. What was my joy when the gates of Paris were opened to see some butter and fresh eggs brought by the hand of a friend, and to receive a remittance from my banker in London, enabling me to discharge all my debts. The sum I had expended was very large, for I told the members of my household never to think of expense if only the absolute necessaries of life could be procured at any price, saying to them, ' We are buying our lives.' In my review of our privations throughout the whole time, I consider that the want of fuel, especially during the intensely cold weather, was one of the severest. When coal failed, and the wood was nearly exhausted, I bought, at an enormous price, a quantity of rafters taken from an old house in course of demolition, and so managed to keep up a miserable fire. All thanks be to God, who has so wonderfully preserved my life!"

Horses must have wonderfully increased in Paris within the last few days. Three days ago I saw for the first time since the siege, three cabs waiting for hire on one of the old cab-stands in the Boulevard des Capucines. The next day I counted nine or ten standing in the Place du Palais Royal, and yesterday there were three or four on the stand at the corner of our street. *Of cats I see none.* I quite miss my old friends who used to lie in a sunny spot in shop windows. They were all caught up during the seige to make "rabbit." If the old proverb be true, " When the cat's away the mice will play," we may expect a great invasion by the mouse species this summer. But, strange to say, although their natural enemies are absent, I have seen neither rat nor mouse since my return, and before the siege they were frequently to be seen near the iron openings to the cellars in our Boulevard Malesherbes, and occasionally were promenading on the asphalt. Some say that when the cunning creatures began to understand that they were considered fit articles for food, they took the hint and disappeared, and have not yet had courage to show their faces again; others that with their natural instinct for finding out well-provisioned places, they left starving Paris for the German quarters, and are not yet persuaded that Paris is sufficiently revictualled to make their way back to their old haunts.

I find, in walking through the streets, that the word "Ambulance," which was to be seen on so many hotels and private houses, is rapidly disappearing, and the red cross is taken down. Let us hope that the poor wounded men are as rapidly recovering. I have been trying to ascertain the reasons of this *émeute* having assumed such proportions. The Belleville insurgents proper do not number more than 60,000, and there are at least 150,000 of the National Guard who have sympathised with this insurrection. The causes are, I believe: 1. The suspicion that the National Assembly wishes to impose a king, and destroy the Republic. 2. The wish for the people to elect the members of the Municipal Council. 3. The unwillingness on the part of numbers of the National Guard to betake themselves to work and lose their thirty sous per day. 4. The question of the payment of commercial bills and rents, which a disturbed state of things will defer. These reasons do not weigh equally with all. With some each one of the four may be the chief cause of sympathy with the *émeute*.

To-day placards on the wall have been plentiful. The first announced the postponement of the elections to Sunday, and the measures of "repression" which the Government intended to take. A while afterwards official announcements informed the soldiers that they had right to the pay of the National Guard, and the National Guard that on giving up their old guns they would receive Chassepots in exchange. Then appeared the protestations of the National Guard, the appeal of the mayors to universal suffrage, next the decrees naming the chiefs of the National Guard, next the protestations of the magistrates expelled from their "mairies," then a third appeal from the united municipalities.

Friday, March 24.

Walking into the Boulevards this morning I found them all quiet, but the shops were still all, or nearly all, shut, and the National Guards were moving about. The Place Vendôme is strongly guarded. Our chapel steward, who has an office in the Place de la Bourse, has just been in, and tells us that the Place de la Bourse is occupied with National Guards, "friends of order," and they are determined not to give up the mairie of the Second Arrondissement in the Rue de la Banque to the insurgents, and that if they attempt to take it there will be a fierce fight. Two battalions from Belleville attempted to come near by two different streets yesterday, but, seeing the strong force of the "friends of order," retreated. There is an uneasy feeling throughout the city which may probably end before night in a terrible conflict.

Two o'clock.—I have been into the Boulevards. The shops were shut; but the omnibuses are beginning to run from the Madeleine to the Bastille. All was quiet. As I passed No. 8, Boulevard des Capucines, I saw the marks made by the bullets of the insurgents on Wednesday. The Rue de la Paix was quite deserted, and only here and there a National Guard to be seen. But the Place Vendôme was full of insurgent troops. Returning by the Rue St. Lazare, I found that the entrance of the Gare de l'Ouest (the railway [right bank] to Versailles) was occupied by the well-disposed National Guards. A temporary wooden railing has been thrown across the carriage entrance, and the entrance for foot-passengers through the iron gateway at the side is kept by National Guards—a wise precautionary measure, as the access to Versailles from Paris might have been stopped—*i.e.*, if the station of the Chemin de Fer de l'Ouest on the south side had also been seized. Great preparations are being made for the elections on Sunday. A red placard is posted on the walls of our arrondissement proposing candidates: " Elections du Conseil Communal.—Jules Allix, publiciste; Arthur Arnould, journaliste; Vaillant, ingénieur civil; Raoult Rigoult." It is supposed, however, that very few in this arrondissement will go to the vote. The mayors have installed themselves in the Place de la Bourse. The houses near the Bourse are all occupied by the " friends of order," who will not hesitate to fire from the windows upon the insurgents if they should invade the " Place."

It appears that acts of pillage are being committed. I have just heard of a man whose box was taken from him in the public streets. To such a condition is this city (the centre of civilisation !) reduced.

March 25.

Things are looking more peaceful this morning. The cafés and some of the shops on the Boulevards are open. The Place de la Bourse is completely filled with National Guards on the side of order. Vice-Admiral Saisset, the Commander of the National Guard, has just issued a spirited proclamation, which was being posted on the walls as I walked along the Boulevards, and he declares that he will defend the cause of order, and the respect of persons and property. In this cause he is ready, if need be, to sacrifice his life, as his only son has already done, in the defence of his country. A barricade has been erected at the end of the Rue de la Paix, and also in the Rue Castiglione, so that the entrance to the Place Vendôme is entirely blocked on both sides; but circulation is free in the streets adjoining, Rue Neuve des Capucines, Rue Neuve des Petits Champs, &c.

It seems very strange to see all the " Bureaux Télégraphiques " in Paris closed. Even during the siege, although the outer world was cut off, it was possible to send telegraphic despatches from one part of Paris to another; but now the offices are entirely shut up.

Saturday Night, March 25.

Paris has continued calm all the day. The announcement was made this evening that the ' Comité Central ' having failed to come to any understanding with the mayors, had decided to proceed with the elections to-morrow. The " friends of order " are mustering in strong force to-night, and there are some who say that there may be a fight in the streets before morning; others think that things are on the point of being arranged. The " proletariat " question, destined to cause so much trouble and anxiety in England, is fighting its great battle in Paris.

Most of the members of the " Comité Central " are members of the *International* Secret Society.

The last news which I gather from the placards on the walls is (1) that some men in the uniform of National Guards have been firing on the Prussian lines : that on examination it turns out that they are former " sergents de ville ;" and that in future anyone convicted of a like offence will be immediately shot. This is the summary announcement of the Central Committee, who also by another *affiche* inform the Parisians that anyone caught in committing theft will be shot out of hand, a notice not altogether destitute of consolation to the trembling inhabitants of the aristocratic quarters, who have heard to their dismay that the prison doors have been opened ; and, although the release from confinement is only granted to political prisoners, it is feared that some marauders may also have escaped. A third placard is from the mayors, saying that an understanding has been come to with the Central Committee, that they have returned to their " mairies," and will proceed with the elections to-morrow. A fourth, signed by six of the Deputies of Paris, exhorting the people to vote to-morrow as the only mode of settling the difficulties of the hour. A fifth is a red bill signed by the members of the council of the International Association, and the members of the Committee of the Federal Council of Workmen, entreating all persons who care for the principles of a real Republic to go to the vote, and assuring them that they will thus secure a

proper consideration of the question of a fair
remuneration for their work, freedom of public
assembly, and the election of their own Municipal Council, without having the officers of the
city imposed on them by a superior authority.
I do not give you the text of these numerous
placards, which involve, if not conceal, their
signification in a multiplicity of words, but have
endeavoured to seize their meaning. I overheard a man in our Boulevard commenting on
the sentence with which Saisset's proclamation
ends, " My device remains that of the sailors,
Honour and Country." " *Patrie ! Il n'y a pas
de patrie ; il n'y a rien.*" " Country ! there is
no country ; there isn't anything." What a
comment is the present state of France on the
passage, " And if a kingdom be divided against
itself, that kingdom cannot stand."

March 27.

As the mayors agreed with the Central Committee on Saturday afternoon that the elections
should be held yesterday, Admiral Saisset resigned his position as Commander of the
National Guard at seven o'clock on Saturday
evening, and returned to Versailles. The
Guards on the side of order at the Bourse and
the Grand Hotel returned to their homes ; and
under the sanction of the mayors, the elections
took place. What is the result, as the bureaux
were kept open till midnight, I have not yet
been able to ascertain. The city yesterday had
all the appearance of being *en fête*. Crowds of
pleasure-seekers were in the Champs Elysées,

and on the Boulevards. One would not have supposed, from the aspects of the streets, that we were in the middle of a revolution! Observing some groups near the gardens of the Tuileries, where the Rue de Rivoli joins the Place de la Concorde, I went up and found men and boys singing the " Marseillaise " to groups of twenty or thirty people, and then offering copies of the words for sale at ten centimes each. The thought occurred to me at once, If this is allowed in one of the most public places in Paris, perhaps preaching in the open air will no longer be interdicted, and there may be means of usefulness open before us in this city which have hitherto been denied.

I found the Boulevards this morning quiet, and many shops are being opened. The Grand Hotel was open, not kept by National Guards, as for the last few days; and although the Rue de la Paix was guarded by pickets, and the Place Vendôme still strongly barricaded, there was the look everywhere of quietness. But how long this is to last, and what is to occur, we know not. Paris is now fairly at the mercy and under the government of the " Commune." These " Red " authorities seem determined to keep order. They declare " death to thieves," and have strictly prohibited gambling as inimical to the real interests of " citizens." The walls of Paris are completely covered with *affiches*— those of the Comité Central printed on white paper, which used always to be reserved for announcements of the Government; the rest being flaring red, the chosen colour of the insurrectionary party. A poster widely distributed yesterday announced that Lyons had followed the example of Paris and adopted the Commune; but we learn this morning that sedition was soon displaced from the Hotel de Ville at Lyons, and that the reactionary party is very strong. Marseilles also has been but little disturbed.

I suppose that now, so far as all practical purposes of government are concerned, Paris is separated from the rest of France. What has become of the old French motto, "*L'union fait la force?*" What will the Assembly do? Leave Paris to itself? or bring up the provincial soldiers to subdue it?

Business seems to be going on to-day, but people have no confidence. There is not a single National Guard either at the Gare de l'Ouest or the Mairie of our arrondissement. Many of the men are tired of soldiering, and are going back to work.

4, Rue Roquépine, Paris.

Monday Evening, March 27, 1871.

I walked this afternoon along the Rue Neuve St. Augustine and into the Rue de la Paix. As I neared the corner where the Rue Neuve St. Augustine joins the Rue de la Paix, I saw a cannon grimly staring out of the barricade along the street, and could look into its muzzle. The barricade was kept by National Guards, who ordered bystanders to move on. Some few were admitted into the Place Vendôme; indeed, I saw numbers of round hats in the very centre of the " Place," mingling with the képis of the National Guards, and no doubt if I had asked I should have been allowed to pass the barricade; but I wished to go along the Rue de la Paix, so contented myself with a good look in the " Place" which still presents a most warlike aspect. Cannons, stacked rifles, troops of National Guards, from the midst of which rose grandly the triumphal column surmounted with the figure of the first Napoleon—such were the salient features of the picture. I took note as I passed along the Rue de la Paix of the points where the victims of the sad massacre of the 27th instant had fallen. The shops were nearly all fast closed; but finding one with the door open I had a long talk with the shopkeeper, a respectable, intelligent man. " These ' friends of order' are really disturbers of order. They had fair notice given them by the sentinels; but they pushed them back, and would not be warned. A man was shot down in front of my shop. I was standing close by and saw him fall. The Central Committee also declare themselves ' friends of order,' and say, ' We mean to make it too." Those reactionists at Versailles want to impose on us a king." "But they say they are Republicans." " They say, yes, but it does not require much perspicacity to see through their acts. Paris has suffered enough from kings and emperors, and means to have a republic. The country, kept in ignorance, has elected the majority of the Assembly. The great towns, more enlightened, hold very different opinions from those held by most of the members of the Assembly. There is now no other course open than for the members of the Assembly to send in their resignation." I passed along the Rue du 4 Septembre. The great letters which I saw chalked up before the siege still remain at the end of the street; but the name has now been regularly adopted, and appears in due form at the intersection of each side street with this new main artery from the Place du Nouvel Opera to the Bourse. As I returned along the Boulevards I saw in a large plate-glass window opposite the Rue de la Paix a round hole made by a bullet on that memorable Wednesday of last week.

March 28.

The city is quiet to-day. National Guards are promenading through the streets, heralded by the bugle and rappel. "Are things on the point of being settled?" I have just asked the shopman in the Rue Royale. "No, they are only just beginning. This state of things cannot last," was his reply. The *Gaulois*, suppressed by the " Comité Central " in Paris, has begun to appear as a single sheet at Versailles. It may be bought on the Boulevards. Some other respectable papers are thinking of establishing themselves at Versailles. The acts of this Central Committee have been singularly at variance with the professed principles of some of its adherents. One of the articles in the political creed of some of the workmen, whose red bill meets you at every corner, is " perfect liberty of the press." This committee, however, deems it prudent to seize the offices of some papers and silence others—their idea of "perfect liberty." Never were more scurrilous journals than some which have recently appeared in advocacy of revolutionary ideas. The *Cri du Peuple* is bad enough, but the worst of all is the *Père Duchêne*. All the papers this morning are full of the results of the elections of Sunday last, which terminated in nearly all the twenty arrondissements in favour of the Red Republicans. But the thing to be noted in connection with the elections was the number of people who abstained from voting altogether. Out of 400,000 electors only 119,000 voted. Arrests are frequent. Indeed, it is dangerous to utter strong opinions against the people now in power. Passages of arms are occurring in the environs of Paris between the National Guards and detachments of the army. Yesterday morning, says the *Moniteur Universel*, a patrol of National Guards of the 66th Battalion, stationed at the Fort Issy, encountered on the plateau of Châtillon a detachment of *Chasseurs à Cheval*, sent from Versailles to make a reconnaissance, and, after exchanging a few shots, the National Guards took to flight.

PARIS UNDER THE RED FLAG.

March 29, 1871.

The roll of cannon of which I spoke in my letter of yesterday, and the purport of which I knew not, turned out to be the salvoes of artillery on the quays near the Hotel de Ville, by which the advent of the Commune was announced to the city. At three o'clock yesterday afternoon battalions of the National Guards from Belleville and Montmartre arrived *en masse* at the Place de Grève, and were arrayed in front of the Hotel de Ville. Other battalions followed, and by four o'clock there were 200,000 armed men in the " Place." Crowds filled the neighbouring streets, the Rue de Rivoli, Avenue Victoria, &c. The names of the candidates elected as members of the Commune were read from the temporary platform erected in front of the " Pavillon de l'Horloge ;" and speeches were made by Assi and Lavalette, which were followed by rounds of applause. Three red flags, one above another, floated from the centre of the Hotel de Ville. The equestrian statue of Henry IV. was covered with red drapery, and served as background to a large bust of the Republic. The enthusiasm of the National Guards was intense. In the evening the Hotel de Ville, the Tuileries, Louvre, and the front of Palais Royal were illuminated. I have this morning walked through the principal streets as far as the Hotel de Ville, to see how Paris looked under the Red flag. The first thing that struck my attention was a placard in the Boulevard, signed by the new mayor of our arrondissement, Jules Allix, in which notice was given of certain meetings of the National Guard obeying the orders of the Central Committee, asserting that France cannot exist without Paris at its head, and advising the members of the Assembly at Versailles to quit *(s'en aller)* as quickly as possible. Turning the corner of the Rue Royale, I saw that the beautiful fountains in the Place de la Concorde were in full play in honour of the new régime. All along I observed that the wants of the city were being well and carefully attended to. Whether it is that "the new broom sweeps clean" I know not, but certain it is that I have never seen the streets of Paris so well swept since the siege as they were this morning. The heaps of rubbish had been cleared away, the centre of the road as well as the causeways well swept, and men were busy watering the roads—a sight very grateful to me, for during the last few windy days I have been almost choked with dust. Arrived in view of the Palace of the Tuileries, I observed that the red flag flaunted over the central "Tour de l'Horloge." How little I thought when taking particular notice of the tricolor flag betokening the presence of the Empress on the afternoon of the 3rd of last September, that the next time I saw a flag floating above the Tuileries it would be the *drapeau rouge*. I found, however, that the red flag brings some advantages, for I was permitted as a *citoyen* to walk along the pavement close to the palace, where I used to see the Emperor pacing to and fro, in company with two or three friends, in other days. The view of the shrubs and trees all decked in the fresh green of the first burst of spring was lovely. Taking my stand in front of the Tour de l'Horloge, I gained the wonderful view, the like of which no other city can boast: first the little fountain in the midst of the Gardens of the Tuileries, with its frame of statues and trees; then the Oberlisk of Luxor in the centre of the Place de la Concorde; then the fine sweep of Champs Elysees, terminated by the Grand Arch of Triumph. All the surroundings were calculated to suggest the idea of a royal or imperial residence, but, turning round, I saw promenading to and fro in front of the principal entrance of the palace, an unwashed National Guard, doubtless from Belleville, whose coat was of the very dirtiest, and whose mien was of the very lowest. Chalked at the side of the grand entrance, in wretched writing, was, "*Republique Française, à la garde des Citoyens.*" Passing out on the quay, I looked up to the wide space over the new entrance to the Place du Carrousel, where was formerly the bronze equestrian statue of Napoleon III. in alto-relievo. On the 5th of September last I saw a large crowd standing here demanding that the statue of the Emperor should be taken down. In place of the statue is now written in large characters, "*République Française, démocratique, une et indivisible. Liberté, Egalité, Fraternité.*" I walked along the quays to the Hotel de Ville. Barges were lying four deep waiting their turn to be unloaded. Barrels and cases innumerable were scattered about in hopeless confusion. Nearing the Hotel de Ville, I expected to be summarily ordered back, but I passed a line of National Guards without hindrance, and found that the barricade which up to yesterday so completely blocked the entrance to the Place de Grève had been partially broken down, and I passed, without being even asked what was my business, into the centre of the Place. It was a sight to be remembered. Along the front of the Hotel de Ville were arranged the cannon, with ammunition. In the centre of the square were numerous groups of National Guards, some answering the word of command, other taking their ease. Now there was the sound of the clarion, and now the roll of the drum. Animation everywhere—a martial scene indeed ! As I walked back along the Rue de Rivoli a man in red Garibaldian costume galloped past on a fiery steed, his sword dangling at his side, and exchanged salutes with red-coated Garibaldians who were walking along the pavement. There was a look in the streets as though men were setting to work again. Indeed, after the *fête* of yesterday the Central Committee urged all to work, and it seemed if their order were being obeyed. In the Rue St. Honoré, a man who had papers to sell was vociferating, " *Le Père Duchêne n'est plus en colère ; il est content.*"

It is said that the Bank of France made yesterday a new advance of 500,000f. to the Central Committee. Under the heading, " *Les Nouvelles,*" the *Petit Moniteur Universel* tells us that the French Government, which ought to have paid to Prussia on Thursday last 135 millions of francs, has obtained, in consequence of recent events, a delay of a fortnight, and that as guarantee for the punctual payment of the indemnity the Prussians are re-arming their batteries and assembling their troops at the north and east of Paris. There seems to be great indignation among the shopkeepers at the present state of things. · Shopkeeper in the Rue St. Honoré : " This cannot last. The Assembly is letting them have their own way for the present, knowing that soon of its own weakness the thing must come to an end. They would have been only too glad if the Government had resorted to violence. They'll get tired of this playing at soldiers. It is utterly contemptible. When one sees them looking over the balconies of the Palace of the Tuileries one is inclined to ask, *D'où cela sort il?* (Whence comes such a creature as that?) Some of them go about in indescribable clothing (*dans un vêtement impossible*). But we have to be careful what we say." At this moment a National Guard came in and the conversation dropped. Shopkeeper in the Rue Neuve des Capucines : " There's no business doing at all. One might as well shut up shop. I should be glad if could I get away from Paris. I don't think the Assembly ought to bring in a king. I have never been a Republican; but just now I think it would be wrong to attempt to establish a monarchy."

Two placards posted on the walls to-day are worthy of note ; one from the Committee of the Commune, announcing that their *affiches* and those of the several municipalities are alone to be printed on white paper ; that no announcement emanating from the Government at Versailles is to be allowed on the walls, and that any infraction of these orders will be severely punished; the other from a proprietor at Montrouge, proposing that all rents between 1,000f. and 2,000f. shall be reduced 10 per cent.; between 2,000f. and 4,000f., 15 per cent.; between 4,000f. and 6,000f., 20 per cent.; between 6,000f. and 8,000f., 25 per cent.; and between 8,000f. and 10,000f., 30 per cent.

March 30.

Paris is still quiet, but no one knows what may happen. There is no confidence, and, say the shopkeepers, less business than during the siege. I observed early this morning two fresh placards; one from the members of the *Comité Central* announcing that having, with the help of the people, well performed their duty, they now resign their power into the hands of the Committee of the Commune, and doubt not that the great object at which they aim will shortly be accomplished, the establishment of a "*République Universelle;*" the other headed *Commune de Paris*, and proclaiming that all the employés for all the "services" must obey their authority, the Commune being the only power *(pouvoir)* now in existence, and that no obedience is to be paid to any orders from Versailles. The Government at Versailles, on the other hand, announces that the employés connected with the administration of the octroi and the employés of the *préfecture de la Seine* and of the *Ville de Paris* were forbidden under any pretext to render their help to the irregular power which has constituted itself at the Hotel de Ville. Both sides threaten forfeiture *(forfaiture)* as the result of disobedience. What are the poor creatures to do?

Reaction is beginning to spring up in Montmartre itself. Here is a copy of a manuscript placard: "The Central Committee gives us fanaticism, hunger, rags, misery. There is no work for the workmen, no industry, no commerce. Is that a good government?" The word *suspect* is making itself known again, as in the times of the first Revolution. Here is a copy of a placard which adorns the walls of Montmartre: "The delegate of the Central Committee charged with the administration of the 18th Arrondissement informs the public that the citoyens (here follow four names) are appointed to receive denunciations against the citizens suspected of complicity with the treacherous Government which has just collapsed at Montmartre." I read in the Paris *Journal* this morning: "Bercy is in consternation. An order from the Committee has just interdicted the export of wines. Every cart loaded with barrels is stopped at the barrier and the invoices are minutely examined. If the buyer is at Paris a National Guard mounts beside the driver and goes to deliver the merchandise; if the buyer is in the provinces the whole is seized and the proprietor referred to the Central Committee." Another paragraph in the Paris *Journal* worthy of notice is: "Yesterday afternoon M. Thiesz, elected in the 12th Arrondissement, presented himself at the *Hôtel des Postes* and asked to speak to M. Ramport. Introduced into the cabinet of the Director-General, he produced an order, signed by the members of the Committee, inviting him to give place to the newly-appointed postmaster. "Sir," replied M. Ramport, " I refuse to obey the Committee. I stay here. If you wish to force me by the use of violence to quit, I warn you that I shall scarcely have quitted my post before all my employés will follow me to Versailles. Paris from that moment will have no more letters from the provinces. Take your choice." Before such energetic language M. Thiesz retired.

Two features of the streets, so different from before the seige, strike me—(1) the innumerable beggars in the principal thoroughfares; (2) the number of invalids, men just recovering from long illnesses, with pale, emaciated faces, and soldiers with arms in slings or with amputated limbs.

This morning I find that the barricades near the Hotel de Ville are nearly demolished. I was in a Bercy omnibus, and expected to get down just before reaching the barricade in the Rue de Rivoli, but the omnibus passed on through the partly demolished barricade and across the Place de Grève. The "Place" was only sparsely occupied by National Guards, and I could move about at my leasure and take a good look at the plaster figure representing the Republic (in front of the statue of Henri VI.) surrounded by five red flags. Between the Hotel de Ville and the barracks were the horses which the Central Committee requisitioned for their artillery. The National Guards seemed to be far more occupied with the question of provisioning themselves than with guarding the approaches of the Hotel de Ville. The good-for-nothing creatures, instead of being at their work and earning an honest livelihood, are eating the bread of idleness, and are now receiving three francs instead of thirty sous per day. Seeing a large shop closed as I walked back along the Rue de Rivoli, and a written announcement posted on the shutters, I went up to read; but instead of seeing "Shut up, disgusted with the Insurrection," I found "*Fermé pour cause de mariage!*" As I passed along the Rue Castiglione and into the Rue St. Honoré I observed that the barricade close to the Rue St. Honoré was down, and that men were at work wheeling away the great paving-stones in barrows to make a barricade near the centre of the Place Vendôme, not far from the iron railings around the triumphal column. Square holes were being left in the barricade for the muzzles of the cannon, from which it is evident they mean still to command the approaches to the " Place." In the Rue de Rivoli I met two or three battalions of the National Guards. A more unkempt lot I never saw. Idle scoundrels! A more thorough contempt than I felt for the lazy rascals as they marched along it would be impossible for any one to experience. The red flag now floats everywhere. Two flaring strips of red are to be seen to-day over the Palais Royal.

March 31.

Dissension soon began to show itself in the councils of the Commune. M. Tirard, mayor of the 22nd Arrondissement, retired, and has written a letter which has appeared in the papers, stating that he supposed the Commune would treat of municipal affairs only ; but, finding that they were intending to discuss political questions also, he immediately retired. Yesterday afternoon the following announcements were placarded on the walls :—

The Commune of Paris decrees

1. The conscription is abolished.

2. No military force, except the National Guard, shall be created or introduced into Paris.

3. All able-bodied citizens form part of the National Guard.

The Commune of Paris, considering that work, industry, and commerce have borne all the expenses of the war, and that it is only just that property should make for the country its share of sacrifice, decrees

1. A general remission to tenants of the rents due for the quarters of October, 1870, January and April, 1871.

2. All the sums already paid by tenants during these nine months shall be deducted from the rent of coming quarters.

3. A general remission also of sums due for furnished apartments.

4. All leases may be cancelled, if the tenants so wish, during the next six months.

5. All notices to quit given by the proprietors may, on the demand of tenants, be deferred for three months.

The Commune of Paris decrees

That the sale of articles pawned at the Monte de Piété is suspended.

I saw several men, who looked as if they were small shopkeepers, reading the second decree with evident satisfaction, and chuckling over the supposed rage and disappointment of the proprietors. In another group gathered round this popular *affiche* I overheard a man saying, " But this is meant only for the people who cannot pay. If anyone who can pay were to take advantage of it to cheat his landlord, I should call him a wretch."

These three decrees show plainly enough the cause of the great strength and popularity of the insurrection. If the Government had been wise it would at once have dealt with the exceptional case of Paris. During the five months' siege the shopkeepers have done scarcely any business. They would now have had their rents to pay to proprietors who have been absent during the siege, and they have not the money to pay them. Most of the poorer people pawned what few valuables they had to get money to live during the siege. Articles precious to them, which they would never have parted with except to buy dear life, found their way to the Mont de Piété. These two decrees therefore are welcomed by a large majority of the population. The abolition of the conscription is also very popular. The indirect blow also struck at the dependence of the Church on the State is rejoiced over by nearly all Parisians.

An announcement is made in the *Liberté* not at all comforting to residents in Paris. " The Chief of the Secret Police of London, now in Paris, says : ' I am assured that there are now in Paris more than 4,000 English robbers who will no doubt search the pockets of the curious who assemble in groups on the Boulevards and elsewhere." It is said that there is to be a grand review of the National Guard by the members of the Commune some day soon, probably in the Place de la Concorde and Champs Elysées. Omnibuses full of clothing for the National Guard are to be seen passing along the streets. Yesterday afternoon at five o'clock I saw, to my astonishment, a flock of sheep and a drove of oxen in the Boulevard des Capucines. Such a sight was never seen in other days at the fashionable hour in the most fashionable boulevard of Paris. *Sic transit!*

Friday, 11 a.m.

I have just learned that no letters have entered Paris this morning, and that the gates are shut. The trains are stopped on some of the lines. So we are shut up as in a cage! As I went out our *concierge* said, "I never felt afraid during the siege, but now I am trembling." Our librarian and his wife both said that the news they heard this morning made them quite afraid.

Evening.

As we are shut in, we thought it would be well to lay in a stock of provisions, and went this afternoon to Potin's, a large provision merchant. The shop was crowded with people on the same errand with myself, and we had difficulty in getting served. One poor woman near us said, "*C'est le dernier jour de notre vie.*" "It's the last day of our life." Others think that affairs will soon be arranged. But who can tell what is to be the end? For myself and those dear to me I have no fear, knowing that we are under the protection of God. Having referred to Potin, let me contradict a statement which went the round of the English papers during the siege, that Potin, a large provision merchant, had committed suicide. The story was that he had concealed a number of hams, and, when they were requisitioned he put an end to his life. The whole story is untrue. He is alive and well. Indeed, he is worthy of all commendation, for, during the siege, when most articles of consumption were sold in Paris at an exorbitant price, he raised his prices very little. The streets of Paris have had a very deserted and sad aspect to-day. It was strange indeed not to see a single postman in any of the thoroughfares.

Saturday, April 1.

I went early this morning to the Gare St. Lazare and the Gare du Nord. At the Gare St. Lazare I found, that although railway communications with Versailles are stopped, the trains still go at the usual hours along the Rouen line, and also to St. Germain and Argenteuil. At the Gare du Nord all was in full activity, and instead of the trains being stopped or reduced in number, I found that a new train to Boulogne had just been added. Our communications with England are therefore not likely to be interrupted, at least not for the present. My next visit was to the Post-office at the Madeleine, which to my joy I found open instead of fast closed as yesterday, and one solitary official walking to and fro. "Have any letters arrived from England?" "No." "Will there be a post to England this evening?" "Yes." "At what time must we post letters?" "Before five o'clock." "Where are the letters that arrived from England yesterday?" "At Versailles." "Where must we make application for them?" "Either at Versailles or at the *Direction Général des Postes*, in the Rue Jean Jacques Rousseau." I came away with a light heart at the thought of postal communications being reopened with England.

The leading article in the Paris *Journal* begins thus: "The Blockade.—Here we are again in the sad days of the siege. Our letters do not leave, our journals are no longer sent into the provinces; our railways even have in part been interrupted. Indeed, the gates of Paris are closed, and the ordinary articles of consumption increase in price. Nothing more is wanted but to see the balloon 'Commune de Paris' rise from the Tuileries, and to hear the cannon roll about our ramparts."

The Commune is making requisition both within and outside Paris. The Palais Royal has been visited by the representatives of the Committee from the cellar to the garret. Seals have been placed everywhere; even the wine has been put under sequestration. To show the complete liberty of the press, the *Constitutionnel* was seized the day before yesterday, and the sale of the *Electeur Libre* forbidden. Several new papers are appearing; among them, *La Fraternité* and *La Sociale!*

April 3.

I walked out yesterday (Sunday) morning along our Boulevard between nine and ten o'clock. At the entrance of the Church St. Augustin I saw great quantities of sprigs of boxwood, and little girls were running about offering the sprigs of green at one sou each. It was Palm Sunday! Nothing different, however, from any ordinary Palm Sunday, except that groups of the National Guard were standing near the pretty fountain in front of the church, and *that the cannon frequently growled in the distance.* We held our peaceful service in the chapel at half-past eleven, and afterwards partook of the Sacrament of the Lord's Supper: God was with us of a truth. The service over, one of our young men, who lives at the Ternes, brought word that there had been fighting at Courbevoie, and that the roll of the cannon was from Valérien. In the afternoon the Champs Elysées were crowded, and large groups of people were to be seen around the Arc de Triomphe standing on the elevated ground or on the projecting stonework to get a view along the Avenue de Neuilly. The wide Avenue de la Grand Armée from the Arc de Triomphe to the Porte Maillot was filled with people and National Guards. After our evening service and prayer-meeting, some of our people gave the following account of what they had heard:—Some battalions of the National Guard had gone out in the direction of Courbevoie, and there had encountered a company of gendarmes and a regiment of Pontifical Zouaves. A skirmish followed, and several were killed and wounded. The battery at Courbevoie kept up a brisk fire during the engagement. The National Guard, finding themselves outnumbered, retreated to the city. In the evening the rappel and *générale* were beaten all over Paris, and the National Guards assembled in great force in the Avenue de la Grand Armée and the district of the Ternes. We say a battalion passing along our Boulevard, going probably, poor fellows, as sheep to the slaughter. And what for?

This (Monday) morning we have heard the roll of the cannon, I suppose from Mont Valérien, since six o'clock. It is now half-past seven, and it still continues. No doubt a fight is going on.

Monday 10 a.m.

The cannonade ceased about nine o'clock, and all has been quiet since. We know not what has taken place this morning; but we hear that National Guards are to be seen walking two and three together along the streets, and looking very dejected. The *Journal des Débats* gives the following account of yesterday :—

"An engagement, which commenced about nine o'clock in the morning, took place between the National Guards stationed at Courbevoie and the advanced posts of the Versailles troops massed for the past few days at Puteaux. At ten o'clock the sound of cannon and mitrailleuses was added to that of the *fusillade*. At eleven o'clock the cannon which had been placed at the *rond point* of Courbevoie ceased their fire. Some shells fell at the entrance of the Bois de Boulogne, near the Porte Maillot. The battalions engaged on the side of the National Guard were the 93rd, the 119th, the 135th, and some companies of the 127th. On the opposite side were some troops of the line and the gendarmes."

The *Liberté* in its account adds:—" Some National Guards beat a retreat, and re-entered the city by the Porte Maillot."

Monday Afternoon.

We cannot get any definite information as to what went on this morning. It is said that the National Guard was compelled to fall back on Paris. The firing of cannon is said not to have been from Valérien, but from the cannon that were placed yesterday near the Porte Maillot. The Boulevards are quiet to-day; indeed, the whole city has a calm aspect, compared with the tumult and effervescence of yesterday. It is said that 160,000 passengers left Paris last week.

This afternoon we walked along the Champs Elysées to the Arc de Triomphe. There was a great concourse of people in the Place de la Concorde and along the Champs Elysêes. Solitary National Guards were here and there surrounded by groups eagerly asking them questions. The poor fellows looked thoroughly fatigued and disspirited. Occasionally a small company of National Guards passed along the Avenue looking quite disorganised. One poor wounded man hobbled along the asphalt leaning on the arm of a comrade with a face the picture of misery, and a clotted stream of blood on his forehead. When we reached the Arc de Triomphe we found it surrounded with crowds of people who were looking in the direction of Courbevoie. Lines of white smoke showed that there had just been a *fussilade* in that direction. The roll of cannon was also heard during the afternoon in the direction of Clamart and Châtillon to the south of Paris.

Evening.

On my return from taking my letters to the northern station, to entrust them to a guard of one of the trains to post them at some station on the line, I met several groups of National Guards returning to their homes at Montmartre, looking fatigued and worn, and covered with dust; so changed in their appearance from what they were when they marched out on Sunday evening. All is very quiet this evening. Such a contrast to the excitement and noise of last night! A woman selling papers at one of the kiosques in the Boulevard, speaking of last night, said : *Je ne pouvais pas dormir du tout. Les régiments marchaient. On criait partout, Aux armes, aux armes.* In to-day's *Journal Officiel* of Paris I read :—

"The Commune of Paris, considering that the men of the Government of Versailles have ordered and begun civil war, attacked Paris, killed and wounded National Guards, soldiers of the line, women and children, and considering that this crime was committed with premeditation and wantonly against all right and without provocation, decrees: Art. I. MM. Thiers, Favre, Picard, Dufaure, Simon, and Pothaun are put under accusation. Art. II. Their goods shall be seized and sequestered until they have been brought to trial before the people's tribunal of justice.

" The Commune of Paris, considering that the first principle of the French Republic is Liberty, considering that liberty of conscience is the first of liberties, considering that the budget of worship is contrary to principle in imposing on people against their own faith; considering, indeed, that the clergy have been the accomplices of the crimes of the monarchy against liberty, decrees, Art. I. The Church is separated from the State. Art. II. The budget of worship is suppressed. Art. III. The so-called benefices of Mortmain, belonging to religious societies, are declared national property. Art. IV. An inquiry shall be made im-immediately concerning such benefices, to state their nature and to place them at the disposal of the nation."

Tuesday, April 4.

The city is quiet to-day, and there seems to be no probability at present of the renewal of the fighting. As I went across the Place de la Concord this morning I saw a group of women assembled around a red flag. Shortly afterwards these women formed a procession, marched along the Rue de Rivoli, and turned up the Rue Castiglione. What was their object I could not make out. A man near me in the Rue de Rivoli, as they passed, said, " Those women are from Versailles, and they cannot get back home, the gates on the side of Versailles being all closed."

Very contradictory statements are made in reference to the doings of yesterday; and as to the accounts given by the National Guards who had been themselves in the affray, each man gave a different story. The papers this morning also contradict each other; but from all we can learn there were three engagements yesterday— one at Nanterre, where some battalions from Ménilmontant and Belleville, under the command of Bergeret, were fired upon by Mont Valérien and dispersed by the shells, which fell into their very midst; another early in the morning not far from Fort Issy, and near Meudon; and the third about three o'clock in the afternoon in the direction of Clamart and Châtillon. In each instance the National Guards, mostly from Montmartre and Belleville were met by a *fussilade bien nourrie;* at first they retired, and afterwards there was a *débandade générale.* The National Guards went home, and show but little enthusiasm for the continuance of the struggle. The loss on the side of the National Guards in killed and wounded was great, some say over a thousand, but it is difficult to ascertain the truth.

April 5.

The situation of affairs remains exactly the same as when I wrote yesterday. We are unable to get reliable news, receiving no English papers; and the French papers in which one has been accustomed to place some confidence (the *Journal des Débats*, for example) have not appeared this morning. But so far as I can learn, fighting is still going on at Clamart and Châtillon. From the top of our tower we can see curling wreaths of white smoke rising from Forts Issy and Vanves, and from the heights of Châtillon, telling that a fierce artillery duel is going on. Sometimes we can hear the heavy roll of the distant cannon. Whether there is also fighting between the troops of the Versailles and the National Guards I cannot tell. Yesterday there was a good deal of fighting near the forts and in the woods, and many wounded were brought into the city. There was much talk yesterday of a probable reconciliation between the Government of Versailles and the Commune of Paris; and it is said that there was a meeting of the Deputies of Paris and the former mayors to strive to be the means of effecting such a reconciliation; but to-day it seems little likely that a reconciliation will take place. Here is the leading article of the *Rappel*:—

" Conciliation ! is it possible between the men who, without declaration of war, attacked Montmartre, who abandoned Paris, who refused the city its rights, who have engaged in civil war, authorise barbarities committed on the prisoners

(The Prussians did not shoot! The Government of Versailles is more savage than the Government of Berlin), who recommence the siege in the presence of the enemy; between these men and the men who took the reins of power after the revolution of March 18, who continue the war, who put Ministers under accusation, who have organised the Commune, who pursue with determination the *reactionaires*, can there be a reconciliation possible? Common sense says No. But is there no method of ending this dreadful situation? Is there no method of stopping the effusion of blood and saving the Republic? Perhaps. On the one side energetic radical measures must be taken; on the other it behoves every one who loves France to devote himself in order to save it. There must be (1) the recognition of the rights of the Commune of the municipality of Paris. (2) The promulgation of a new electoral law, assuring to the different towns of France—to the different Communes—a more homogeneous representation, which will prevent their votes from being swamped by the country votes, which will guarantee, in a word, the rights of the intelligent and enlightened minorities. (3) The dissolution of the Assembly at Versailles, and the convocation, as soon as possible, of a Constituent Assembly. (4) Re-elections everywhere. At this price Paris may be satisfied, and the civil war may be stopped. But let this be done quickly, for blood is flowing." This article is signed "Edouard Lockroy." Paris is looking sad and deserted. About half the shops on the

Boulevards are closed, and some only half open. What is to be the end it is difficult to predict.

April 7.

We are truly again in the " Reign of Terror." Many have been arrested and imprisoned, and there is a general feeling of uneasiness throughout the city. The guillotine was set up on the Boulevard Voltaire, but it was immediately burned, and I hear two accounts, one that it was burned by the indignant people, another that it was brought out from the prison de la Roquette and burned purposely to show the people's horror of capital punishment. There was heavy fighting in the direction of Courbevoie yesterday morning and afternoon. There was a terrible fusillade on the bridge of Neuilly, and the bridge and barricade are now in the hands of the Versailles troops. Three positions near Paris are now occupied by the troops, Asnières, Courbevoie, and Puteaux. There are different reports as to the number of killed and wounded in the combat of yesterday, but it is agreed on all hands that it was very great on the side of the insurgents. A National Guard said to-day, " *Nous serons bientôt écrasés.*" (We shall soon be completely destroyed.) There was a great concourse of people at the funeral of the National Guards who fell on the 3rd, 4th, and 5th. The procession passed from the Hospital Beaujon along the Boulevard Hausmann, Boulevard Malesherbes, and along the line of the Boulevards de Madeleine, des Capucines, &c.,

to Père la Chase. The bodies were conveyed in three funeral cars draped in black, with red flags at each corner. Several battalions of the National Guard followed, the men looking thoughtful and sad. At intervals there was the sound of the muffled drum. The procession was followed by men and women, relatives and friends of the deceased. Dense crowds lined the Boulevards on each side throughout the whole course of the procession. It was an impressive sight.

Fighting has been going on again to-day at Neuilly. I could see the bombs from Mont Valérien quite plainly from the Arc de Triomphe. The Champs Elysées were crowded throughout their whole length with people going up to see the battle from afar. Oh that these days of civil war may speedily come to a close !

A meeting was to have been held last evening in the Salle de la Bourse, but it was interdicted. An announcement to this effect was placarded yesterday. " The Commune of Paris decrees, Art. I. The meeting announced for this evening at six o'clock, Salle de la Bourse is interdicted. Art. II. Every manifestation likely to disturb order and to excite intestine strife during the battle will be rigorously repressed by force."

Nevertheless, from the leading article in the *Journal Officiel* of Paris this evening, it seems as if the Commune were giving way a little :—

" The Government of Versailles deceives you in saying that Paris wishes to govern France and exercise a dictature which would be the negation of the National Sovereignty. They deceive you when they say that robbery and assassination are publicly perpetrated in Paris. Our streets have never been more quiet." (This is true enough, but it is on the principle, "Make a desert and then call it peace.") "During three weeks not a single robbery has been committed! Not a single attempt at assassination has occurred. Paris only aspires to found the Republic, and to acquire its communal franchise, happy to furnish an example to the other Communes of France. If the Commune of Paris has gone beyond the circle of its normal *attributions*, it is to its great regret, and it has been only to answer to the state of war provoked by the Government of Versailles. Paris only aspires to govern itself, full of respect for the equal rights of the other Communes of France. As to the members of the Commune, they have no other ambition than to see the day arrive when Paris, delivered from the Royalists who threaten it, will be able to proceed to new elections."

We are in doubt as to whether Paris will be again bombarded, and have to endure the horrors of another siege. It appears, from what has transpired in the Assembly of Versailles, that there are many of the deputies who would be glad to see Paris bombarded and the city burnt to the ground. They seem to forget that burning Paris would not destroy the weeds they are striving to uproot, which would crop up elsewhere if turned out of their favourite soil in Paris. The cause of this tumult lies deep, and cannot be dealt with at a stroke. This " proletariat" controversy, which is at the bottom of all, is the great question for the next generation to settle. A significant paragraph has appeared lately in some of the papers, showing that for the same room occupied by a workman the rent has been *trebled* within the last eighteen years. The notion, right or wrong, that the workmen are spending muscle and brain to enrich capitalists, without getting a corresponding increase in wages in proportion to the increasing value of their labour, is laying hold of the whole class of workmen.—All feel very acutely the being cut off from correspondence with friends. We are told that now all letters put into the post are forwarded, but we have received no letters since March 30.

There is an order published by the Commune that all citizens from seventeen to thirty-five years of age are to enrol themselves in the National Guard. Yesterday there was a great crowd of people at the Northern Station flying from Paris. National Guards were there in force, preventing any man who could not bring proof that he was a married man and not within the age in which he would be liable to serve, from leaving Paris. There never was, in the history of the world, a despotism like that under which we are living. Well may we say, with Madame Roland when she was being led to execution in 1793, " O Liberty, what crimes are committed in thy name!" One good thing will have been accomplished by these days of terror; a wholesome hatred of the Commune will have been inspired into the minds of the people.

In addition to the arrests of the Curé of the Madeleine, &c., we hear that the Curé of St. Laurent and many priests at the Jesuits' College have been arrested and incarcerated. The valuables of the churches have been put under sequestration. Many Roman Cathalic churches were shut up to-day.

April 8.

At three o'clock this morning I heard the roll of cannon, and it continued till seven or eight o'clock. There was then a slight cessation. Afterwards during the morning there was the occasional boom. It seems that yesterday a bomb fell at the corner of the Arc de Triomphe and another in the Avenue Josephine. The city is now regularly besieged, though not invested. The Versailles troops are drawing nearer the fortifications; they occupy the bridge of Neuilly and part of the Avenue de Neuilly. The ramparts are being bombarded from Valérien, and possibly an assault may be made to-morrow.

The representatives of Paris present at Versailles have addressed a declaration to the inhabitants of Paris in the interests of peace and order, deploring the useless effusion of blood, and lamenting that, while the enemy is still on the soil of France, the blood of Frenchmen should be shed in civil war. Whether this "declaration" will produce an effect remains to be seen. In the *Journal Officiel* of Paris this morning is the following paragraph:—

" Considering the patriotic *reclamations* of a great number of National Guards, who, although married, hold to the honour of defending their municipal independence, even at the price of their life, the decree of April 5 is thus modified: From seventeen to nineteen years of age the service in the companies of war shall be voluntary, and from nineteen to forty obligatory for National Guards, whether married or not. All good patriots are expected themselves to form the police of their arrondissement, and to force the refractory to serve."

Here is the account of yesterday which appears in *La Petite Press* :—

"The action was concentrated at Courbevoie and at Neuilly with even more fury than before. What cannonading! At the moment we arrived at the Arc de Triomphe, exactly three o'clock, the crowd, an immense crowd, was flying in all directions in the greatest disorder, men, women, children—everybody was running in the direction of the Champs Elysées and the neighbouring streets. 'What is it?' we asked. 'Ah, Sir,' replied an old man, 'a bomb has fallen in the avenue on this side the *enceinte;* hence the panic that you see.' From this point the bombs did not cease to rain on the Porte Maillot and the fortifications. So far as one could judge from this distance, the Versailles troops were massed at the foot of the column of Courbevoie. Their batteries, six in number, were placed in front of the column, firing upon the barricade of the bridge of Neuilly and upon the barrier of the Porte Maillot. At four o'clock the barrier was demolished. Some National Guards crossed the road running, and took refuge in the houses on the left side. The batteries of the fortifications fired without interruption; nevertheless, the Versailles batteries evidently drew nearer. The struggle was more severe than ever. One could count by hundreds the projectiles which were hurled against the wall of the *enceinte* and in the avenue at about 160 yards from the Arc de Triomphe. Mont Valérien mingled its hoarse voise in this horrible concert, sending its shells to the right and to the left, as if the movements of the National Guards were taking place outside the fortifications. One heard from time to time the frightful grinding of the mitrailleuses."

The general aspect of the streets, except the Champs Elysées, is the same, deserted and gloomy. The *partie officielle* of the *Journal Officiel* contains this announcement: " Considering that the grades of generals are incompatible with the democratic organisation of the Guard, and were only temporarily used—Art. I. The grade of general is suppressed. Art. II. The citoyen Ladislas Dombrowski, commander of the 12th Legion, is named Commander of the place of Paris, instead of citoyen Bergeret, who is called to other functions."

Monday morning, April 10.

Yesterday (Easter Sunday) morning was ushered in with the roll of cannon. The quiet of our morning service was often interrupted by the heavy clap caused by the explosion of the bombs near the Arc de Triomphe. All was comparatively quiet during our evening service and the prayer-meeting which followed. Some people came to us during the day to ask where they could find shelter, as shells were falling around their houses. It seems that during Saturday night and throughout yesterday the houses situated in the Avenue de la Grand Armée and Avenue des Ternes suffered a continuous bombardment. Mont Valérien fired at intervals, and the batteries at Courbevoie thundered without intermission. The shells fell mostly in the Avenue de la Grande Armée and around the Arc de Triomphe, one injuring the arch just above the bas-relief on the right hand. Some shells fell in the neighbouring streets, Rue de Galilée, corner of the Rue de Berri, &c., and one is said to have reached the Parc Monceaux. Many have been the victims of the bombardment. Women and children have been killed or wounded. A wine merchant was killed close to his own door, and a *chef de musique*, by name Thibaut, was so severely wounded that he died a few minutes afterwards. A shell fell on one of the chains surrounding the Arc de Triomphe, sending the rings far and wide. One of them wounded a poor man in the leg. Indeed so dangerous did it become in the afternoon to go near the arch that no one was allowed to pass along the Champs Elysees beyond the Rond Point. Below that point, however, there was an immense crowd. True, some faces seemed much saddened and solemnised; but the greater part seemed to have come out as a spectacle! Will it be believed when death, havoc, and destruction were being dealt out wholesale within so short a distance, that a goat carriage drawn by four goats was to be seen near the asphalted walk, and the people near seemed to take pleasure in the diversion! A perfect anomaly is the French character. At five o'clock yesterday afternoon some National Guards began to throw up a barricade at the junction of the Rue Royale with the Place de la Concorde. As there are no paving stones in the Rue Royale, the work of raising a barricade was more difficult than in other places where paving-stones are at hand, and the work went on but slowly. There was hardly any firing to be heard last night, and this morning when I went out, about seven o'clock, all was perfectly still in the streets. No progress had been made with the barricade at the end of the Rue Royale; but as I stood in the Place de la Concorde I saw two companies of National Guards, with pick-axes and shovels on their shoulders, making towards the corner of the Rue Royale and the Rue de Rivoli. They immediately set to work. By twelve o'clock these two barricades, composed principally of earth thrown up from deep holes cut in the road, were completed half across each street. From these preparations it would seem as if an attack were still expected, as certainly was the general belief yesterday. The aspect of the city to-day, and the silence of Valerien and of the batteries of Courbevoie, except an occasional detonation, lead me to think some efforts must be in course of being made at Versailles to effect a reconciliation.

The news reaches us that Thiers in the Assembly has contended for the municipal freedom of all the towns in France, and that if his point were not conceded, he would retire from his post as Chief of the Executive power. Surely if this be granted, and it should be tolerably certain that the Republic will be maintained, there will be a basis of conciliation, and this civil war may be brought to a close.

Most of the priests taken prisoners within the last few days are still detained, but one or two have been set at liberty. Among those released may be mentioned the Curé of St. Eustache, who was allowed to leave his prison yesterday morning. When he appeared in the pulpit at St. Eustache the men waved their hats and the women their pocket handkerchiefs. The Archbishop of Paris, so say the papers, has been removed from the Conciergerie to the prison Mazas. Rumour says that M. Duguerry, the Curé of the Madeleine, an old man of seventy-six years, most highly esteemed and beloved throughout his parish, has died in prison, overwhelmed with grief and chagrin. Notre Dame was entered and pillaged yesterday. Nothing, however, of great value was found. 1793 did the work of pillaging Notre Dame so thoroughly that there is but little left for 1871 to do. Several domiciliary visits have been paid; but in very few instances has much spoil been found. The Curé of the large church close by us, St. Augustin, and the Curé of La Trinité, at a short distance, have both been placed under arrest. The Curé of St. Laurent managed to escape.

Thousands are flying from Paris. Scarcely a young man, except in the uniform of the National Guard, is to be seen. The '" *Laissez passer* " must be procured at the Prefecture of Police in order to leave Paris, and no man between nineteen and forty years of age is allowed to quit. It is stated that 50,000 persons left the city each day last week. From the deserted look of the streets, if it were not for the magnificence of the houses, one would suppose oneself to be walking through a second-rate provincial French town.

A devoted English lady, Miss Blundell, who love the French and has spent years in France in earnest efforts to do them good, has just printed a fly-sheet in the style of *Père Duchêne* beginning " *Ils sont venus !*" and ending with an earnest exhortation to sinners to come at once to Christ. She was *suspecte* of favouring the Versailles party, and marched off between two armed National Guards. But when her fly-sheet was read through it was pronounced to be " *irréprochable*," and she was set at liberty.

We see here and there in the streets great waggons filled with furniture with *Déménagement* in large characters upon them. It would seem as if the people remaining in Paris were meaning to take advantage of the decree of the Commune absolving them from the payment of rent for the last nine months. Some on leaving their apartments have had the impudence to ask their landlords for a receipt for the amount of their rent !

Elections for the vacant places in the Commune were to have taken place to-day; but a placard posted this morning announces that they are deferred. *Père Duchêne* (the ultra-Communist paper) says, that this putting off the elections is worse than a crime, it is a fault! and declares himself for the first time in absolute opposition to the Commune. Bergeret, the former *Commandant de la Place de Paris*, is now under arrest. So much for the concord of the Commune!

3 p.m.

On looking out from the top of our tower in the direction of Neuilly and towards Issy, Vanves, and Montrouge, I see much white smoke, showing that my hope that hostilities were ceasing is vain. The last news is that the cannonade and fusilade still continue at the Porte Maillot, and that an attack is being made on Montrouge.

Paris, Monday evening, April 10.

Going out about four o'clock this afternoon, I was surprised to find the Boulevards, the Rue Royale, the Rue de Rivoli, the Place de la Concorde, and the Champs Elysées as far as the Rond Point, crowded with people. But remembering that, being Easter Monday, it is a general holiday, one could, under ordinary circumstances, have accounted for the great concourse of people; but surely none except French people would have turned out for a holiday when such numbers of their fellow-countrymen are at this moment lying dead or wounded. Crossing the Place de la Concorde, we found a great crowd gathered around the Obelisk of Luxor, looking up the Champs Elysées. No bombs, however, were flying about to-day, as yesterday, and we could see that some venturesome people were walking up to the arch. There was another crowd along the Quai de Billy. The object of their curiosity was a collection of gunboats, seven or eight in number, moored alongside the quay, but with their steam up and ready to start at any moment. The *Opinion Nationale* this evening has an article headed "*La Paix! la Paix!*" and gives an account of the interview of the delegates of the commercial men in Paris with M. Thiers. I hear that the Versailles cannon has broken the *pont levis* of the Porte Maillot, and that at any moment the Versailles troops might enter. The preparations now being made by the National Guards indicate the expectation of street fighting. In addition to the barricades recently constructed at the end of the Rue Royale and the Rue Rivoli, we saw, when in the Place de la Concorde this afternoon, that they were making a strong barricade at the entrance of the Pont de la Conde. If it should come to street fighting, the slaughter would be terrible.

An amusing paragraph in connection with the Northern Station is going the round of the papers : " The Prussians are not confining themselves to interdicting any interference on the part of the members of the Commune with the management of the Northern line. They have, to a certain point, taken possession of the Northern Station. For two days a Prussian officer, dressed in ordinary costume, has taken up his abode in the bureaux of the station master, and superintends the regular departure of the trains. At nine o'clock an individual strangely attired, with a grey hat and waistcoat *à la Robespierre*, drove up to the station in a carriage with four horses, and escorted by four red-shirted horsemen. He asked to see the station master, and said that the Commune, of which he was a member, held him (the station master) responsible for having allowed more than 200 men between seventeen and thirty-five years of age to leave Paris by that line. 'Sir,' said the station master, 'I do not recognise the Commune, and besides, the Northern line is placed under the surveillance of the Prussians, and to them you must address your complaint.' At this juncture the Prussian officer made his appearance, and requested the member of the Commune to follow him. 'Where? Who are you?' 'A Prussian officer, about to transport you to St. Denis.' Without further delay the whole party set off at a gallop."

The following letter appeared in the *Times* of April 15th :—

April 12.

In the omnibus last evening, as I went to the Chemin de Fer du Nord to find some passenger to take my letters to England, was a woman talking to a National Guard about the losses in

killed and wounded during the last few days.
The number was spoken of as being very great.
One battalion had been almost entirely cut up.
The woman at the end of the conversation
uttered a deep groan, more significant than any
words she could have employed. As we were
sitting quietly in our room at 9 o'clock last
evening we heard the loud report of a gun, as if
very near, then two more detonations, and then
immediately succeeded what seemed to be a
terrible fusillade, and it appeared so near that
we supposed it must be in the Champs Elysées,
and we came to the conclusion that the Versailles
troops had come in by stealth, and that a fierce
battle was raging between them and the insurgents within a short distance from us. We
opened our windows and looked out. The night
was very dark; and on the black sky, apparently
just over the Palais de l'Industrie, was a lurid
glare, flashes exactly like lightning glinting the
heavens. We first fell on our knees to pray to
God to have mercy on the poor creatures who
were at that moment being killed; then we
mounted our tower, and from this excellent point
of observation watched the battle till midnight.
At 10 o'clock the firing slackened, and the hoarse
grating of the mitrailleuses was less frequently
heard; but the cannon growled more furiously,
and it seemed to us as if it were within the city.
Had the Versailles troop entered? Were they
gaining the victory or not? If within the city,
how had they entered? were questions which
agitated us, but which we could not settle. At
midnight we retired to rest, and slept as well as

the report of artillery at intervals would allow us. From 5 to 6 there was a constant cannonade. Before 7 I was out and got the *Petit Moniteur Universel* and the *Vérité*. From them we learnt that the battle had been at Issy, that the Versailles troops had surprised the advanced guards of the insurgents, who had retired under the protection of the guns of the forts. 11 a.m. —The cannonading still continues from Neuilly, Mont Valérien, and the forts on the south side of the city, but is less vigorously kept up than last night. We learn that Asnières was again the scene of conflict yesterday. The Versailles troops occupy the houses towards Courbevoie, but the insurgents have most of the village, and are strengthening their fortifications at the railway station. Several bombs have fallen in the streets, but as yet little damage has been done. I trust our little chapel, which is close to the station, has escaped injury. It escaped during the siege only to be placed in greater danger now. In viewing Paris from our tower I observe a strange feature. In the days of the Empire no smoking chimneys were allowed in this beautiful Paris, but now I see several tall stacks, like those of Birmingham or Sheffield, rising from the midst of the houses. I find they are from the workshops for the manufacture of cannon, and if I may judge from the great volumes of smoke they send forth to blacken the sky and give the dismal tinge, the mark of London respectability, to the neighbouring houses, this manufacture must be carried on with great activity just now. We hear this morning that the managers of the Northern station have been arrested, and that there is a probability of the trains being stopped. Sad news to us, implying the entire cessation of our sending letters by passengers to our friends. I hope it is not true. More *curés* have been arrested. The Conciergerie will soon be a conclave of priests. Yesterday several men were surrounded by armed National Guards and forced to arm and join the insurgents. One poor man at Montmartre, a member of our French congregation, who would probably have been taken off, found refuge here last night. The Freemasons of Paris have placarded the walls with a protest in the name of humanity against the continuance of this civil war, and have sent delegates to Versailles to strive to be the means of negotiating a reconciliation. The bombardment of Paris from Mont Valérien still continues. A shell fell this morning in the Boulevard Haussman, not far from the Parc Monceau. Great indignation is expressed against M'Mahon, who entered on his duties as Commander-in-Chief of the Versailles forces yesterday, and, it is thought, wished to signalise the fact by carrying the southern forts. Sedan was to be revenged on Paris, and M'Mahon was to wash away the dishonour of Sedan in the blood of Parisians. From all we hear the Prussians are likely to put in an appearance on the scene if this sad business is not soon settled. General Fabrice is said to be at St. Denis, Prince Frederick Charles at Compiegne, and German troops are massed all around the north and east of Paris, some of them stationed within five minutes' walk from the ramparts.—3 p.m. Cannonading is still continuing at Neuilly, and evidently, from the loud report, with large pieces. Issy and Vanves are also firing occasionally. The two arms of the cross surmounting the Pantheon have been cut off, and a red flag is to be seen floating on the summit of the building. It has ceased to be a church, and is again dedicated, as in 1793, "*aux grands hommes.*"

April 13.

Last evening, about half-past nine, we heard again the din of battle—the fire of musketry and the rattle of mitrailleuses. On looking out we found it was much further off than the night before. About ten o'clock the artillery began to play an active part, and the roll of cannon mingled with the rifle-firing. The night was not so dark as the night before, but the sky was partly overcast, and the flashes of light glittered here and there on the sombre clouds. We learn this morning that the attack was made by the Versailles troops on the outposts beyond the southern forts, mostly in the direction of Clamart. The fusillade ceased before eleven o'clock, but the sound of cannon was prolonged through the night. I slept well nevertheless, and awoke to the same boom as I heard just before falling asleep. Going into the Place de la Concorde about seven o'clock, I found a company of people near the Obelisk looking up the Champs Elysées, the upper portion of which near the arch was dimmed by smoke. Bombs are still falling around the arch and in the neighbouring streets.

11 a.m.

We hear heavy firing towards Neuilly and Courbevoie. It is said that the troops and the National Guards have come to hand-to-hand fighting, the two opposite sides being in adjoining houses and fighting from garden to garden and from house to house.

Fighting still goes on at Asniéres, and Mont Valérien sends shells upon the village. Some houses suffered severely yesterday in the Rue de Bretagne, close to the new chapel. We are in great anxiety as to its safety. Several shells have struck the Arc de Triomphe, occasioning, however, but little damage. The statues representing the principal French towns in the Place de la Concorde still keep the black covering over their faces. They may well mourn over poor France! Nantes alone, the black covering thrown across the shoulder, looks with calm mien towards the garden of the Tuileries, now bursting out into the fresh green of spring. The trees along the whole line of the Champs Elysées are beginning to be beautiful. The weather is fine, and the temperature mild; everything to make the city enjoyable if it were not for this horrible civil war. With the return of spring might have come the return of happiness and prosperity were it not for these internal discords. Alas! when will they cease? From much that I have seen and heard I am forced to the conclusion that many of these fellows of Belleville and Montmartre, finding themselves with arms in their hands, are determined to go on with the game of fighting, and, other enemies failing, no matter to them, they will fight their own countrymen. Many of them know not what they are fighting for. I don't wonder that just now so many Frenchmen are ashamed of their nationality.

We saw yesterday on the Boulevard de la Madeleine, one of the most fashionable parts of Paris, what I never expected to see in the centre of the metropolis of France—a man in the middle of the broad asphalted pavement, with a crowd around him, performing feats with heavy weights, lifting them and throwing them over his head; a sight such as you might see on the green of a provincial village on a *fête* day. Paris, the gay, the fashionable, is reduced to this. The empty state of the city—*i.e.*, as far as carriages are concerned, has, however, some advantages. One can cross the Boulevard reading a newspaper all the time without any fear of being run down. Fancy this in the Strand or Cheapside.

In the *Siècle* this morning is the copy of a letter written from the prison de Mazas on April 8 to the President of the Assembly, begging him to seek to end as soon as possible this civil war. I find that the report that M. Duguerry, the Curé of the Madeleine, had died in prison is incorrect. *He* also writes from the *Depôt de la Conciergerie* to the members of the Government at Versailles, begging of them not to allow any executions of wounded or prisoners, as such executions excite great anger in Paris, and might produce terrible reprisals, a resolution having been formed, at the occasion of each new execution at Versailles, to order double the number of the hostages in their hands to be put to death.

A paragraph from a speech delivered by Thiers in the Chamber of Deputies in 1840, during the discussion of the project for fortifying Paris, is placarded on the walls and signed " *Un Ami de l'Ordre.*" " What ! to imagine that these works of fortification could injure liberty or order is to place oneself out of all reality. And, besides, it is to calumniate a Government, of whatever kind it might be, to suppose that it could some day seek to maintain itself by bombarding the capital. What ! after having pierced with its bombs the dome of the Invalides or the Pantheon, after having inundated with its fires the houses of your families, would it present itself to you to demand the confirmation of its existence ? But it would be a hundred times more impossible after the victory than before."

An announcement of the Commune posted this morning informs the inhabitants of Paris that the museums are shortly to be opened to the public, and the usual annual exhibitions of modern paintings is to be held ! Will it be believed that when on Tuesday night we were listening, transfixed with horror, to the din of the battle, some French people were looking out from the windows of a neighbouring house on the rolling fire that seemed to pierce the very heavens, were bursting into roars of laughter !

A battery has been placed in position on the Trocadero to attack Valérien. We may therefore expect in reply more shells from Valérien in the interior of Paris. The managers of the Northern Station, imprisoned two or three days ago, have been set at liberty. We may therefore hope that the train towards England will not be stopped.

Evening.

This is the day so much looked forward to by the friends of order in Paris as a day of deliverance. The general report was that, if the Government had not reduced Paris to subjection before that day, the Prussians would enter the city on the 15th. But the day has come to a close without the fulfilment of these hopes. There has been, however, terrible cannonading all day, as if an entrance were being forced. While we met in our quiet prayer meeting this evening, we had the heavy roll of the cannon in our ears. A fierce fusillade has also been going on during most of the afternoon and evening in the direction of Neuilly. We can get no reliable information as to what is really transpiring, and can only, comparing what we see and hear, come to our own conclusions.

The Protestant establishment of the "Diaconesses" for the sick and infirm was entered a day or two ago by some agents of the Commune. They made diligent enquiries and searched the whole place, entering at ten o'clock at night, and not leaving till six o'clock the next morning. At last they went away without having found anything of importance to lay hands upon. The only thing taken away was a watch hanging on a wall. The man who took it, being remonstrated with, replied, "If I don't take it, some one else will." The Curé of St. Roch has been arrested and imprisoned. The parishioners in the Rue St. Honoré are in a state of great indignation about it. The large church near us, St. Augustin, has been closed for several days. What makes everyone so full of fear in these troublesome times is that numbers of men under the name of the Commune go about to pillage. The bombardment, although not carried on vigorously the last two or three days, still makes its victims. A family at the Ternes, living near the top of a house, and through the illness of the father of the family unable to remove, had a shell sent into the midst of their little apartment. Two of the children were killed, the mother wounded. The youngest child and the sick father escaped unhurt.

The investment of Paris on the south side is said to be complete, and we are in some doubt as to whether the battles of the last few nights, which here are said to be attacks by the Versailles troops, have not been repulses of sorties made by the insurgents. Another idea we have is that, if they were attacks made by the troops, they were made with the design of drawing the insurgents away from the forts and then surrounding them.

Placards issued by the Commune still abound on the walls. One announces the adoption by the Commune of all the wives and children of men who die " in defending the rights of Paris." Wives, " married or not," are to receive 600 francs a-year ; children, recognised (*i.e.*, legitimate) or not, 365 franc a-year, parents or other relatives who can show that they were dependent upon those who have died, from 100 to 800 francs, according to circumstances. These words, " married or not," " legitimate or not," are worthy of note as showing the idea entertained by Communists of the sanctity of the marriage bond. Tacitly, though not openly, a general divorce is pronounced under this dreadful rule of the Commune. Another placard signed by Cluseret, *délégué à la guerre*, tells that he has examined all the positions and finds them satisfactory, that Versailles has summoned them to surrender in the space of twenty-four hours. " Let the powder reply," is the concluding sentence. A third placard conveys some comfort to inhabitants of Paris who have been in constant dread of a domiciliary visit from robbers under the name of National Guards, declaring that no perquisitions will be allowed except those ordered by the Commune, and their order will always be stamped at the "*Ministère de la Guerre.*" The National Guards are commanded to watch and see that no other perquisitions are made. We have therefore the comfort of knowing that if we are robbed it will be by authority ! The same want of truth which has distinguished the official announcements under the different administrations ever since July last still shows itself in the placards of the Commune. The attacks of the enemy are always repulsed. The losses of the *fédérés* are always small. Although everyone knows that the number of killed and wounded has been very great every day on the side of the insurgents, it is officially declared in a despatch signed *Cluseret* that on the 13th the loss was " five wounded and two killed."

With the storm of war around, a storm of thunder, lightning, and hail burst over the city this afternoon. The sound of heaven's artillery was a pleasant change after hearing for days this horrible din of civil war.

Paris, April 14, 1871.

We are truly under a " Reign of Terror." A woman, formerly a servant in our family, came yesterday and told us that her husband had been taken off by some National Guards and forced into a *Compagnie de Marche* three days ago, and she had heard nothing of him since. He had hidden in the cellar till he could hide no longer. Two National Guards had come into their apartment, one armed with a revolver, the other with a Chassepôt, and had threatened him if he would not go with them. When he referred to his wife's unwillingness to let him go, they turned to her and threatened to shoot her. " Shoot me, then," said the woman. However, the end was that the poor man was forced to go. So much for the liberty enjoyed under the rule of the Commune.

The following paragraph has appeared in *Galignani's Messenger* :—" Notification of the British Embassy. Mr. Malet, second secretary of her Majesty's Embassy, deems it right to repeat the notice published by Lord Lyons on the 13th of last September, and to declare that British subjects who continue to remain in Paris now do so at their own risk and peril, and that those who delay their departure may find themselves hereafter unable to get away."

The three delegates of the "*Ligue d'Union Républicaine des droits de Paris,*" just returned from Versailles, have published the result of their interview with M. Thiers. These are the main points :—

1. M. Thiers guarantees the continuance of the Republic.

2. Paris is to have the same privileges as other towns in France.

3. The Government will proceed to an organisation of the National Guard, but will not admit the principle of the absolute exclusion of the army.

4. All who give up the armed strife, and enter peacefully their homes, shall be exempt from prosecution. Only the assassins of Generals Clement Thomas and Lecomte, if found, will be judged according to the law.

5. The National Guards will continue to receive their pay for several weeks.

Surely this is all these people can demand. The three delegates are to have an interview with the members of the Commune to-day.

The fighting yesterday was principally at Neuilly. The insurgents advanced on the right side of the avenue nearly to the bridge. The Versailles troops still held the houses on the left side. The Versailles batteries at the Rond Point de Courbevoie and the cannon planted at the Porte Maillot and at the Porte des Ternes kept up an artillery duel throughout the day: Mont Valérien fired both on the Porte Maillot and the new battery of the Trocadero. Many shells fell on the houses at Passy. Some poor women and children were killed, and the inhabitants fled into the safer parts of the city, not at all grateful for the establishment of the battery so near to them. All seemed quiet in the evening, but at ten o'clock gleams of light were to be seen on the hills of Châtillon, and about one o'clock in the morning there was the sound of battle—the report of musketry and the growl of the mitrailleuse.

The din of war I heard in the dead of the night was, it seems, an attack by the Versailles troops on Vanves. What was the issue I find it difficult to ascertain. The losses are said to be great on both sides.

7 p.m.

There has been comparative quietude all day. We have scarcely heard the cannon at all. There has been everywhere a feeling of uneasiness, as if either a terrible assault were about to be made or that we should be shut in to the horrors of another siege. In the middle of the day I received by post a copy of the circular already quoted from *Galignani's Messenger*, sent from the British Embassy. I made my way to the Embassy to know what it meant, and found that, as the bombardment of the city had begun, and it was probable that before long blood would be shed in the streets, the Secretary had deemed it right to issue such a notice to the British residents in Paris. I learned to my great joy, that Lord Lyons has sent word that British subjects may send and receive their letters through the Embassy.

In walking through the streets of Paris I see numbers of English flags. I had no idea there were so many English families in Paris. Where are they all on the Sabbath-day? Certainly not in the churches. On this question of the English in Paris, I have lived long enough here to learn that there are numbers of English people who have given up English habits, dismissed English ideas, and are English only in name, and when something is to be gained by showing their nationality. The difficulty of labouring among such people is very great. They hide themselves away from their fellow-countrymen, and become French in their thoughts and modes of life. English ministers may labour here for years without even being able to find them out. But when such times as these come, forth go their English flags. There is also a. class of very poor English people in Paris, scattered over the city. whose very existence is altogether unknown until something occurs to throw them to the surface. Such are those who, during the siege, made their way in numbers to the British Charitable Fund.

Another feature of the streets just now is the number of couriers on horseback—*estafettes*—who ride along at full gallop carrying messages to and from the members of the Commune. The proprietors of the Grand Hotel are making use of this time, when there are so many strangers in Paris, to cleanse the hotel thoroughly after its occupation as a hospital during the siege. Painters, whitewashers, and upholsterers are at work, so that, when things are a little more settled than at present, and the former *clientèle* of the Grand Hotel return, they may take up their abode without fear in their old quarters.

M. E. de Pressensé and M. G. Monod, Protestant pastors, have both written to the *Temps*, protesting against the imprisonment of the Archbishop of Paris and other priests, and begging for their immediate release.

9.30 p.m.

Fighting is now going on in the direction of Châtillon. While I write I hear the noise of battle, the hoarse roar of the mitrailleuse, and the boom of the cannon. The sky towards the south is at intervals completely lit up, and gleams with flashes like forked lightning.

Saturday morning, April 15.

We learn that the fighting last night was another skirmish between the advanced guards on both sides near Meudon. There has been heavy canonading all night, both at the south of Paris and at Neuilly.

Monday, April 17.

On awaking yesterday (Sunday) morning our ears were greeted with the same awful noise of cannon, and it continued all through the day till evening, when there was a short cessation. The quiet of the morning service, as on Sunday last, was interrupted by the booming of cannon. Immediately after we joined in the prayer of the Litany, " That it may please Thee to give to all nations unity, peace, and concord," there was a tremendous burst from a siege gun, which almost covered the responses ot the congregation. After the service, Pastor E. Cook came in, just arrived from Jersey. He had come *via* Granville, Versailles, and St. Denis. At Versailles he had seen one of the Députés, whose report was that " things are progressing slowly." Pastor Scheffter also called, and told us that he had been yesterday in our chapel at Levallois (the chapel specially under his care), and a rifle ball had come through one of the windows and flattened itself on the opposite wall. He picked up the ball, and at the same moment another ball came, and he had a narrow escape of being hit. He thought it prudent to immediately leave the chapel. Mr. W. M. Taylor, who was present at the service, told us that, a day or two ago, having occasion to send a load of goods along the Avenue des Ternes, the poor driver had been killed by a shot from a mitrailleuse, and the cart was besmeared with blood. We had comparative quiet, for which we were very thankful, during the evening service and the prayer meeting which followed. As we retired about eleven o'clock all was still, or nearly so, and we hoped for a night undisturbed by the hateful roll of war, when suddenly the same now too familiar noise of a fussilade, in the direction of Neuilly, began again, and continued for some time. There was canonading all through the night, and it continues this morning. But, if we may judge by the sound, it is the cannon of the fortifications, probably spending ammunition uselessly. I find to-day three new placards, the first signed by Cluseret, and giving an account of yesterday, of course telling of a victory, and that the Pontifical Zouaves, with the gendarmes and the sergents de ville, were vigorously combated at the Church of Neuilly and repulsed; the second announcing that a court martial had been instituted, composed of six members, who will sit in permanence to try the numerous cases awaiting judgment, the cases of capital punishment to be referred to the Executive Council; the third requiring all arms to be given up at the respective *mairies*, and ordering the disarming of all refractory National Guards. It is said that Dombrowski has been wounded in the neck, and that thus he may be disabled from commanding for a few days. A word, in speaking of Cluseret and Dombrowski as to the character of this insurrection. Both the military leaders are foreigners. Cluseret is of French descent, but, banished in 1848, he went over to America and became a naturalised American, and took part in the American war. Dombrowski is a Pole, or, as some assert, a Russian, who was sentenced to Siberia, but managed to escape. Both these men are said to be capable leaders, but neither of them is a Frenchman. So of the men under their command, although the majority are Frenchmen, there is a fair sprinkling of Italians of the Garibaldi school, and of Englishmen of the ultra-Red Republican party. It seems as if it were generally understood that this is a great struggle between the *plebs* and patricians, and the partisans of the *plebs* are rallying around the standard of Red Republicanism. I may be wrong, but it seems to me this *Emeute* has gained its strength and consistence from its connection with the International Secret Society.

Although the city is not really invested, the question of supplies is beginning to be a serious one. Country people don't care to bring their provisions into a city bristling with cannon and abounding in barricades. Naturally prudent, they prefer to sell their provisions to the Prussians, who surround the city on the north and east, and to the French who surround it on the south and west, to running the risk of penetrating into the city at the risk of losing their lives by shells or bullets. Hence, the price of provisions is rising rapidly. Veal, which sold at 1f. 40c., now sells at 2f. the pound; leg of mutton, which a week ago was selling at 1f. 30c., is now 2f. 90c. At the last market of La Villette there were only 600 oxen. Our butcher said that in a week's time there would be no more beef to be had. These insurgents are, I believe, well provisioned, for I have seen for the last fortnight immense quantities, in vehicles requisitioned by the Commune, passing through the streets of Paris, as if they were going to some place of safety to be stored for the use of the Commune. The sufferers now, as during the time of the siege, will be the poor inoffensive people who have had nothing to do with the *émeute*, but who, living in the same city with the *émeutiers*, suffer for their folly and wickedness. "Woe is me that I sojourn in Mesech, that I dwell in the tents of Kedarf."

The interior of Paris presents an aspect more and more sad. The streets, the boulevards, have completely changed their look. Everywhere there is emptiness and solitude. Even the Boulevard des Italiens, generally the centre of animation, is deserted. The shops are mostly closed, or only half-opened. When I talk with the shopkeepers about the state of affairs I only have one reply—a deep sigh and "Pauvre France!" Groups of people are to be seen at all hours of the day at the end of the Champs Elysées, near the Place de la Concorde, watching for the explosion of bombs. Some venture along the avenue as far as the Rond Point, and a few more during and imprudent than the rest go as far as the Arc de Triomphe. The arch has been injured in twenty-seven places. Long will Paris bear the marks of this revolution.

Accounts reach us on all hands of the terrible results of the bombardment in the district of the Ternes, especially between the Avenue des Ternes and the Avenue de la Grande Armée.

Shells have fallen the last two days in great numbers. The poor frightened people take refuge in the cellars, but even there are scarcely safe. Balls, too, whistle about in all directions. Two men were talking quietly together in the Avenue des Ternes, and were both of them wounded. " Spies " are being arrested in numbers. A young man near the Arc de Triomphe was arrested on Saturday because he was looking with a *lorgnette* in the direction of Neuilly. On Friday six persons were seized in the Avenue d'Eylau because they were looking towards Mont Valérien, and their gestures made some National Guards believe they were making signals to the fort ! The members of the Commune, making believe that they are very careful of the lives of citizens, have just issued an order that the couriers *(estafettes)* are not to gallop along the streets, lest they should endanger the lives of citizens. I wish they were equally careful of exposing the lives of citizens upon the battle-field.

4 p.m.

The cannon still rolls and the bombardment goes on. Mr. ———, who has just called, tells us that this morning a pastrycook, standing at the door of his house in the Avenue des Ternes, was killed on the spot by a shell. A bill posted on the wall announces that since yesterday all the gates on the north and east of the city from the Porte de Clichy to the Porte d'Orleans are open from 6 a.m. to 6 p.m., and free ingress and egress allowed without *laissez passer*, except for men between 19 and 40 years of age. Another bill tells that the parks and public gardens, closed since the beginning of the siege, are to be opened from 6 a.m. to 7 p.m. They are making excavations at the junction of the Rue de Rivoli with the Place de la Concorde, but whether to construct barricades or for some other purpose I could not understand.

April 18.

The more I get to know about this insurrectionary movement the more I am convinced that it is a great effort of the Red Republican party in Europe to gain their ends. They have been on the look-out for years for a field of operations; they could not find it in England or Germany, but in Paris, at this particular juncture, they have found exactly what they have long wanted. And to make their cause more popular they have turned the legitimate desire on the part of the Parisians, to have the municipal management of Paris in their own hands, to suit their own nefarious purposes. Two entirely distinct things have been blended together. Hence Paris gets blame which she does not deserve. The Assembly is angry at Paris. The anger and complaint should be directed against that which Paris happens to contain at the present moment. The " word of order " to these people in Paris is said to come from the International Society in London! These are questions in which all Europe is interested. Unfortunately poor Paris has to suffer because she is the scene of strife. The scum of Europe has been collected in Paris to fight out this battle. I have never seen such countenances, not even · typified in Madame Tussaud's Chamber of Horrors, as are now to be seen in Paris. An artist with a powerful pencil might get many a hint for a new edition of Bunyan's " Pilgrim's Progress " if he were now in this city. "Old Adam," " Hate-good," " Malice," " Love-lust," " Liar," " Cruelty," " Enmity," " No-good," " Envy," all find their most expressive representations in faces which may be said to be " types of sin."

I happened to meet Pastor William Monod this morning. He was evidently sad at heart because of the multiplied troubles of his poor but dear country. He spoke of the foreign element in the insurrection as a partial excuse for his own countrymen.

We heard last night that great numbers of the insurgents had been surrounded and taken prisoners between Asnières and Mont Valérien. Our *concierge*, having had to go to Batignolles, heard the *rappel* and *générale* everywhere and the *clairon d'alarme*. The cry " *Au secours* " was general. So we did not know whether to believe the report; but this morning the news is confirmed, not in the papers, which maintain a significant silence, but from lip to lip; the following particulars being added, " A whole battalion from La Chappelle taken prisoners. Of another battalion only the commander returned, all the rest taken prisoners. A third battalion almost entirely cut up. Some *wagons blindés* also taken by the Versailles troops." It is generally supposed that a simultaneous attack will be made on all the sides of the city occupied by the French. The *rappel* was but faintly responded to at Batignolles last night, and even those who did make their appearance in answer to the call seemed much discouraged, and showed no heart for the fight. All these are welcome signs of the coming termination of the struggle. In the meantime, however, preparations are being made for the street fighting. Passing along the Rue de Rivoli this morning, we found out the reasons of the excavations at the point where the Rue de Rivoli joins the Place de la Concorde. It was the erection of a barricade after the new fashion ordered by the Commission of Barricades—a deep trench to be cut on each side the barricade and filled with gunpowder, the barricade itself in the centre constructed not of stones, but of earth. They were this morning throwing up another barricade in the Rue Castiglione. The Commission of Barricades also orders by a placard on the walls, after giving directions for the construction of the barricades, that gunpowder shall be placed at certain intervals in the drains. If it were possible, these desperate fellows, rather than yield, would blow up Paris. Happily, such a catastrophe is not possible. Yet the fact of their undermining the city with gunpowder is not at all comforting to timid people. I passed along the Rue de Rivoli, and saw, to my joy, that the decree of the Commune that the Column Vendôme should be demolished has not been carried into effect, nor is the scaffolding erected, as was reported. I believe we owe the preservation so far of this historical monument to Cluseret, who induced the Commune to delay the execution of their decree until " the termination of hostilities," which, of coure, is putting it off indefinitely.

The result of the elections on Sunday to fill up the number of members of the Commune is now known, and shows that they created but little interest, only about one-eighth of those inscribed having voted. Requisitions are still being made. The house of the Brothers Pereire in the Faubourg St. Honoré has been visited, and all the wine in bottles, some of it worth 25f. a bottle, carried off. The Belgian Embassy in the Faubourg St. Honoré has also been invaded by some of the National Guards. This, however, has created such an outcry that the offenders have been arrested and imprisoned. I know not whether they will next come to us. I have put out the British flag in front of the chapel, and given orders to the *concierge*, should any of these roughs make their appearance, to summon me at once. It is a comfort at such a time to think that we are English. By the way, let me tell you that the British Embassy has been of great service to the few British subjects remaining in Paris. Lord Lyons kindly allows us to have our letters brought from Versailles in the bag of the Embassy. Let me cite another instance of kind consideration on the part of the Embassy. An English professor now has a situation at Morlaix, Finistere. His wife, also teacher of English, finding little to do at Morlaix, made her way to Paris after the termination of the war. Shortly after the outbreak of the revolution she made her way to London. In the meantime, however, her husband, finding that postal communications were stopped, and anxious to send some money, wrote to Lord Lyons asking his lordship to supply his wife with necessary funds until postal communications were reopened and he was able to repay the money advanced. Last evening I received fifty francs from the Embassy to meet this case, which, as the wife is now safe in England, I have taken back this morning. These isolated cases, small in themselves, will suffice to show that the British Embassy is now caring for the British subjects still in Paris, and regaining the esteem which it lost by having no representative of England at the Embassy during part of the siege. By the present abnormal state of things a complete stop has been put to work of nearly all kinds, and most of the workshops are closed. The Commune, in their short-sighted wisdom, have ordered that the workshops that have been abandoned shall be re-opened for the benefit of the co-operative societies of workmen, as though the opening of the workshops would bring back the work! The violation of private houses is now permitted under authority, under pretence of searching for arms *chez lez émigrés, réfractaires* or disbanded National Guards. A letter in the *Opinion Nationale*, signed H. Lassimoune, gives an account of his being arrested at Passy, on the 6th of April, for posting a placard announcing a meeting. He was brought before a tribunal of four citizens, one of whom, as soon as he entered the room where the trial was to be held, pointed a revolver at him, and said "I'll blow out your brains." When the citizen became a little more calm the trial proceeded, and ended in his imprisonment at the Prefecture of Police. At the end of four days he was unexpectedly released.

We are all hoping for a termination of this terrible civil war by compromise, to avoid the further effusion of blood; but we know not how it is to be brought about. Thiers is willing to make concessions, not to the Commune, with whom he cannot treat, but to Paris asking to administer its own affairs. Whether these concessions are such as Paris will accept is matter of doubt. It would be wise, however, to consider the demands fairly; for if Versailles succeeds in quelling the insurrection, the demands, if not met in a liberal spirit, will crop up under another form; whereas, if they are granted so far as they are just, Paris may hope for peace and quietness for some time to come.

We see to-day two new placards of the Commune, one announcing that the professors at the School of Medicine have deserted their posts, and asking for medical men as volunteers to supply their lack of service; the other issuing an order to all the Gardes Sédentaires to give up their chassepots for an inferior weapon, in order that the *Compagnies de Marche* may be supplied with proper arms. An appeal is made to their patriotism to perform this duty, a hint being given that if they do not voluntarily give up their chassepots, they will be forced to part with them.

Neuilly is in sad plight ; some of the houses burnt, most of them riddled. Some parts of the Ternes near the fortifications have not fared much better. The firing has been much slacker to-day. I hope that this is a sign we are near the end of hostilities.

We are beginning to find the result of the partial blockade in the rapid rise of prices. The supplies at the *Halles* are falling short, and at the market at La Villette there is only one-fourth of the amount of sales effected at this time last year. True the population of Paris has been much reduced by the large number who have fled, but that emigration will only partially account for the failure of the supply, and we may expect prices to rise higher day by day.

5.30 p.m.

We hear that there was fighting again at Asnières this morning, and that the insurgents sustained serious losses. In the *Mot d'Ordre*, Rochefort's paper, it is said that *pourparlers* are being exchanged between the two parties.

April 19.

The least sign of the possible termination of this civil war is welcomed. Hence I read with pleasure that a deputation from the town of Lyons has waited on Thiers, and has also sought an interview with the Commune. I was not sorry also to read in the *Bien Public* that in the Faubourg St. Antoine, which used to be the hot-bed of Red Republicanism, there is a general discouragement among the National Guards. Those who marched willingly at first, thinking they were fighting for the municipal franchise, now see that the Commune is going further, and that success is impossible, and many of them are relinquishing the strife. The same symptoms are manifest at Batignolles, where the great majority of the Guards say that they have had enough of it. These short extracts from the *Opinion Nationale* afford food for reflection : " The situation of Paris is such that no one can believe himself in security, either for his liberty, or for his goods, or for his life ;" and, " The Prussians in Paris, such is the necessary final result of the part to which the Commune seems to have committed itself." The sad effect of the present state of things on the material happiness and prosperity of the people is everywhere apparent. Shopkeepers are in evil case : scarcely a customer is to be seen in the shops. Hotels, which at this time of the year are generally so full, are empty. Those frequented by foreigners, and especially those favoured by English people, are deserted. Yesterday, in passing the Hotel Meurice, which has been for so many years a home for my countrymen, I saw that, instead of the usually wide-open carriage way into the court, inviting the welcome traveller, the great doors were closed. The number of beggars, reminding one of Naples as it used to be under the Bourbon rule, had become so great in the public thoroughfares that even the Commune has found itself obliged to take the matter in hand, and, by placards posted everywhere, has forbidden begging in the streets.

From the accounts in the papers this morning we learn that the scene at Asnières on Monday was terrible. The bridge of boats having been broken in the middle by order of the *chef de légion*, Landowski, in order to stop the retreat of the 77th and 125th battalions, the first ranks already on the bridge, to prevent themselves from being pushed into the water by those who were following, threw themselves flat on the bridge one above another. In the frightful disorder which followed numbers of the poor fellows fell into the water and were drowned. Yesterday, although we did not hear so much noise because of the change of wind, Valérien and the new batteries in the Parc de Neuilly and the Château de Bécon kept up a constant fire all through the day. Shells fell in showers on Levallois, on the railway bridge at Asnières, and in the district of the Ternes. A bomb fell very near the Ternes Chapel, but did not touch the building. In the next street to the one in which the chapel is situated, Rue Bayen, a mother of four little children had her head carried off by a shell. The poor little children were covered with fragments of plaster, but were not killed. Many other sad casualties are reported. My heart bleeds at the recital of horrors of which I hear.

Rain has fallen plentifully during the last few days, and has much discouraged the insurgents!

This may seem strange to English people, but any one who has lived in Paris knows full well what an effect is produced upon Parisians of every grade by a few drops of rain! Numbers of the insurgents, it is said, have bronchitis and lumbago, and are only too glad to go home and get cured. They have more fear of inflammation of the lungs than of shells! Butcher's meat is becoming very dear; 1s. 7d. per pound is asked for and given for rib of beef.

11.30 a.m.

I have just been to my point of observation on the top of our tower. The forts on the south, Issy, Vanves, and Montrouge, are all quiet. So is Valérien; but I hear some *coups de canon* and *coups de fusil* in the direction of Levallois. The people at Passy have reason to be thankful that the Trocadero battery has ceased, as it drew on them the fire of Valérien. The reason of its having ceased was thus given in a placard posted on the walls, and signed by Cluseret: "The battery at Trocadero has reached the buildings of Valérien, and inflicted appreciable injuries. That was all it was desirable to ascertain for the present." The fact is, that the shells from Trocadero never went further than Suresnes, and the harm they inflicted was not on Valérien, but on the poor defenceless people of Suresnes, some of whom were killed in their houses.

The way from the Rue de Rivoli to the Place de la Concorde is now blocked by the barricade. Vehicles have to make the détour by the Rue St. Honoré. The wind during the last day or two has been too strong for the strings by which the black covering was tied on the faces of the statues representing the great towns in the Place de la Concorde, Lille and Bordeaux, after having been blinded for six weeks, gaze again on the beautiful fountains; and even Strasbourg looks out above the crowd of *immortelles* by which she is covered. Large red posters have been placed on the walls this morning, containing an extract from a speech delivered by Thiers in the Chamber of Deputies in January, 1848, to this effect: " Palermo has been bombarded. And by whom? By its own government. And what for? For demanding its rights. Such an event may well excite the indignation of Europe. Lille, fifty years ago was bombarded by the Austrians; Copehagen by the English; Barcelona by the Regent Espartero. In each case general indignation was aroused."

The following is the version given by one of the moderate party as the reason why the friends of order did not rally in greater force at the outbreak of the insurrection : " I am a man of moderate means, a *calligraphe* (penman), gaining my livelihood by my own exertions. To pursue my calling I am obliged to live near the centre of the city. I have an apartment in the Boulevard Poissonière. I remained in Paris during the siege, became one of the National Guard, and did my best to defend Paris, encountering with my fellow-citizens exposure in performing my duties as National Guard, and also the privations of the siege. In order to live, I was obliged to sell some '*obligations*,' the fruit of my economy for years. These '*obligations*' I had bought at 300f. each, and was obliged to sell them at 50f. each. After the siege, not having earned a sou for seven months, I was expected by my landlord to pay the arrears of rent on the 12th of April. I pay 3,000f. a-year for my apartment. The rent used to be 1,200f., but within the last few years has been raised by the landlord to 3,000f. My landlord, like most other landlords, was away from Paris during the siege. After the 18th March, when the insurrection broke out, I belonged to the *parti d'ordre*, and joined those who rallied around the standard of order at the Bourse. One day, on entering my apartment, I received from the *concierge* a paper. On opening it I found it was a *congé* (notice to quit) from my landlord. I threw my sword to the other side of the room, and there it is still." This question of rents has had much to do with the course events have taken during the insurrection. Respectable people have said: "Why should I trouble myself? Let the landlords come and fight their own battle." There is a general feeling that Paris, having suffered exceptionally during the siege, ought to have been the first consideration of the National Assembly.

It is said that 500,000 persons have left the city since the 18th March.

Thursday Morning, April 20.

There was a general expectation last evening that an attack would be made during the night by the Versailles troops. We saw several companies of our National Guards marching along our Boulevard towards the Asnières gate. The *rappel* was beaten till late in the night. However, we heard nothing further than the heavy roll of cannon kept up all through the night and continuing this morning. I see a placard on the walls, " Dombrowski à l'Exécutive,' dated yesterday, 19th April, and telling that all was going on well at Montrouge and Asnières—the enemy repulsed—his right wing advancing—some of the advanced posts of the Versailles troops almost surrounded; but he wanted a reinforcement of 2,000 men immediately, as the enemy was in strong force.

A notice appeared in the *Journal Officiel of the Commune* announcing the suppression of four papers : *Le Soir*, *Le Cloche*, *L'Opinion Nationale*, and *Le Bien Public* appeared nevertheless last evening, each containing a protest against the Tyranny of the Commune.

The law of the Commune on the question of *échéances* (bills falling due) has been promulgated, allowing the suspension of payment for three years!

Neuilly, Levallois, the Ternes, and Asnières are still suffering a continual bombardment. A shell fell in the school play-ground connected with the Ternes Chapel, yesterday, but the building itself still escapes, although bombs have fallen all around. The Commune has made an offer to exchange the Archbishop of Paris for Blanqui, imprisoned some time ago by the Government, but it has been refused.

In the midst of all this turmoil we continue our services, and they are truly times of refreshing. On Tuesday evening a few of us held a special prayer meeting to plead with God for the termination of this civil war. Last evening we held our usual service, followed by the class-meeting, and found that, according to his Word, Christ was present with the " two or three."

Thursday Evening, April 20.

To-day at noon immense placards were posted on the walls, of which the following is a translation : " Declaration of the Commune to the French people. In the sad and terrible conflict which imposes once again on Paris the horrors of the siege and bombardment, which causes French blood to be shed, which dooms to destruction our brothers, our wives, our children, crushed under shells and shot, it is of prime importance that public opinion should not be divided, that the national conscience should not be troubled. It is necessary that Paris and the entire country should know what is the nature, the reason, the end of the Revolution which is now taking place. In a word, it is just that the responsibility of the griefs, the sufferings, and the misery of which we are the victims should fall on those who, after having betrayed France and delivered Paris to the foreigner, seek, with a blind and cruel obstinacy, the ruin of the great city, in order to bury, in the disaster of the Republic and of Liberty, the double witness of their treason and their crime.

"The Commune considers that it is its duty to affirm and define the aspirations and wishes of the population of Paris: to explain the character of the movement of March 18, misinterpreted, misunderstood, and calumniated by the political men who sit at Versailles. This time again Paris works and suffers for the whole of France, of which it is preparing, by its combats and its sacrifices, the intellectual, moral, administrative, and economical regeneration, the glory and prosperity. What does it demand? The recognition and consolidation of the Republic, the only form of Government compatible with the rights of the people and the regular and free development of society. The absolute self-government *(autonomie)* of the Commune extended to all the parts of France, and assuring to each the integrity of its rights, and to every Frenchman the full exercise of his faculties and capabilities as man, citizen, and workman. The self-government of the Commune will only have for limit the right of equal self-government for all the other Communes adhering to the contract, the association of which will assure French unity. The inherent rights of the Commune are the vote of the Communal budget, implying the control of receipts and expenses; the fixing and division of taxes; the direction of local services; the organisation of the magistrature, of the interior police, and instruction; the administration of the goods belonging to the Commune. The choice by election, with the permanent right of control or recall, of the magistrates and public functionaries of all orders.

The absolute guarantee of individual liberty, of liberty of conscience and liberty of labour. The permanent intervention of citizens in the Communal affairs by the free manifestation of their ideas and the free defence of their interests, the Commune alone being charged to watch over and assure the free and just exercise of the right of public meeting and publicity. The organisation of the defence of the city and of the National Guard, which shall elect its own chiefs, and alone watch over the maintenance of order in the city. Paris does not wish for further local guarantees on condition, be it understood, of finding in the great central administration, the delegation of federated Communes, the realisation and practice of the same principles. Paris, however, reserves the right of making the administrative, and economical reforms that its population may claim, to create institutions suitable for the development of instruction, production, exchange, and credit, to regulate power and property according to the necessities of the moment, the wish of those interested, and the rules furnished by experience.

"Our enemies deceive themselves or deceive the country when they accuse Paris of wishing to impose its wish or supremacy on the rest of the nation, and of pretending to a dictation which would be a veritable menace against the independence and sovereignty of other Communes. They deceive themselves or deceive the country when they accuse Paris of pursuing the destruction of French unity, constituted by the Revolution in the midst of the acclamations of our fathers assembled at the fête of the federation of all the parts of old France. Unity, such as has been imposed on us up to this day by the Empire, by monarchy, and parliamentarism, is only despotic, unintelligent, arbitrary, and burdensome centralisation. Political unity, such as Paris wishes, is the voluntary association of all local initiatives, the spontaneous and free concurrence of all individual energies in view of a common end, the well-being, liberty, and security of all. The Communal Revolution, begun by the popular initiative of March 18, inaugurates a new political era, experimental, positive, scientific. It is the end of the old governmental and clerical world, of militarism, of monopolies, of privileges to which the proletariat owes its servitude, the country its miseries and disasters. Let this dear and great country, deceived by lies and calumnies, be reassured. The struggle between Paris and Versailles is one of those which cannot be terminated by illusory compromises. The issue cannot be doubtful. Victory, pursued with unconquerable energy by the National Guard, will rest on the side of right. We summon France as witness. Let Paris, under arms, possess as much calmness as bravery; let it maintain order with as much energy as enthusiasm; let it be willing to endure sacrifice with as much reason as heroism; let it only be armed through devotion to the liberty and glory of all, that France may cause this bloody conflict to cease. It is for France to disarm Versailles by the solemn manifestation of its irresistible will. Called to benefit by our

conquests, let her declare herself the associate of our efforts ; let her be our ally in the combat which can only end in the triumph of the Communal idea, or by the ruin of Paris ! So far as we are concerned, citizens of Paris, we have the mission of accomplishing the modern Revolution, the greatest and the most fruitful of all that have illumined history. It is our duty to struggle and conquer. "The Commune of Paris.
" Paris, April 19, 1871."

The hope that the Column Vendôme would be spared is, it seems, to be doomed to disappointment. In the papers to-day it is announced that the materials composing the column in the Place Vendôme are offered for sale in four lots—two lots materials and construction ; two lots metals. *La France* this evening gives a list of forty-seven priests arrested between the 1st and 18th April ; twenty-six churches closed since the beginning of the month, among them Notre Dame, La Trinité, St. Philippe du Roule, St. Roch, and Notre Dame de Lorrette ; and a list of twenty-four " *Maisons Religieuses* " and convents, in which perquisitions have been made. I happened to-day to meet an English chaplain, and I find he takes a very gloomy view of the present aspect of affairs. and counsels all English people to quit Paris. He has seen several members of the Commune, and finds that they are determined to fight it out to the end ; that probably it will come to street fighting, and then the struggle will be dreadful ; that the Commune is getting help from other countries, numbers of foreigners daily coming into Paris, and among them many Englishmen of Red Republican principles.

The boom of cannon and the occasional sound of musketry have been heard all day in the direction of Neuilly and Asnières, and shells have been rained on the Ternes. Three bombs fell to-day in the Faubourg St. Honoré, in the garden of the Rev. Mr. Forbes, the chaplain of the English Church in the Rue d'Aguesseau, and they have sought a safer abode for the time in the interior of the town. A fragment of a shell has broken into the roof of our Ternes Chapel, and scattered the plaster, but has done no further injury. Shells are also still falling around the Arc de Triomphe, and in the Avenue d'Eylau. Will it be believed that, notwithstanding, a wedding took place in the Avenue d'Eylau, and that some of the wedding party ran to pick up the fragments of a bomb that exploded near them!

Friday Morning, April 21.

There has been heavy cannonading all night, and the hoarse noise of the mitrailleuses. There was fighting throughout the whole of yesterday from Neuilly to Asnières, and the noise in that direction this morning confirms the news that the combat is continued to-day. The positions of the combatants have not materially changed. There is a general idea, however, that an attack in considerable force by the army of Versailles is imminent. Report says that in any case the Commune is doomed, for, if the Versailles troops should be repulsed, the Prussians will take the matter in hand, and establish a respectable Government.

Friday Evening, April 21.

A bomb has fallen in our boulevard (Boulevard Malesherbes) near No. 107, close to the entrance of the Parc Monceau, not so near as to cause us much disquietude, but still quite near enough! *La Ligue de l'Union Républicane des droits de Paris*, notwithstanding the failure of its effects hitherto, does not seem to be discouraged. This morning a great red placard was to be seen everywhere, containing their new address. They announce that they maintain their former programme, and will take resolutions, following the different phases of the strife, which may appear to them the best fitted to assure the triumph of their principles, and that they are now resolved to place themselves in correspondence with the municipal councils of the principal towns in France, and to let them know the legitimate wishes of Paris, to which they will lend their support.

I fear the constant sight of warlike preparations will exercise a most baneful effect upon the youth of this city. I see mere children marching in rank and file along the streets with sticks in their hands or across their shoulders, and one of them blowing a horn. Scarcely a boy is to be seen in the streets without his gun-stick. No doubt numbers are saying to themselves, "*Je serai soldat.*"

I think the Commune are beginning to find out that it has been a mistake to force unwilling men to fight. In many regiments only one-fourth have fought from conviction or with heart; the rest have only marched from fear or for the pay. Hence the *morale* in many of the battalions has been very low. Said a man to me the other day, " Yes, of course, if I am forced I shall march; but *I shall never fire*, or if I fire, it will be in the air, or with blank cartridge." Another man, who was in the battles on the south side of Paris on the 11th and 12th, said that he fired his gun *in the air* so as to be sure of not killing anyone, and that he wore his ordinary clothes under his regimentals, so that, if a chance offered, he might fling away his regimentals, and either escape or go over to the opposite side. This accounts for so much noise, and, happily, so little fatal result in some of the skirmishes.

A bill has been posted this afternoon with a new Order of the Commune—(1) that all cafés, concerts, theatres, and public establishments shall be shut from half-past twelve to six a.m.; and (2) that any such places that may be found favouring gambling and prostitution shall be immediately closed.

I passed along the Rue de Rivoli to-day, and saw the barricade at the entrance of the Place de la Concorde, and the one in the Rue Castiglione, both of which are assuming quite a formidable appearance. The barricades around the Hôtel de Ville have also been greatly strengthened.

Saturday, April 22.

The account this morning is that there was fighting yesterday, as before, at Neuilly from house to house, and also at Levallois, neither side gaining any great advantage. Dombrowski sends word to the Executive that "the enemy is in retreat!" The seventeen omnibuses and carriages filled with dead bodies. which came in at the Clichy gate, to say nothing of the ambulance waggons bringing wounded men, do not afford convincing proof of the truth of Dombrowski's despatches. The suppression of the four journals two or three days ago has exasperated many Republicans against the Commune. It is a common thing to hear people inveighing against the tyranny under which Paris is now groaning ; but they say, " What can we do ? Felix Pyat, one of the members of the Executive, lifted up his voice boldly in the *Vengeur*, and said that the suppression of newspapers is always dangerous and useless. Whether on this point of the suppression of newspapers dissension has shown itself in the Commune I know not, but I find that the seven names which, as *the Executive*, have been hitherto appended to all official proclamations (Cournet, Felix Pyat, Tridon, Vermorel, Delescluse, Avrial, Vaillant), appear no longer, and that a new Executive Commission has been appointed.

2 p.m.

In going towards the Palais Royal I saw a bill containing an appeal to all natives of the

French Departments in Paris to meet this afternoon in a large room at the *Arts et Métiers* to hear an address in favour of "conciliation." The barricades at the corner of the Place de la Concorde and in the Rue Castiglione are assuming the appearance of miniature fortresses. In the Court of the Palais Royal an awkward squad of workmen in blouses was at drill. A young Englishman residing in Paris, whom I happened to meet, said that the current opinion was that a great attack by the Versailles troops was expected within the next week, and at the same time by the insurgents a blow-up of some of the streets, and a general pillage!

We had a visit while I was out this (Saturday) afternoon from two National Guards, who asked what this building was, and to whom it belonged. On hearing that it was English, they said "*Bon*," and departed.

Chantilly, Paris Circuit, April 27, 1871.

On Tuesday, April 25, during the time of the armistice, I took my wife and family out of Paris, and placed them in safety here at Chantilly. The Northern Station was filled with armed men, whose duty was to prevent any Frenchman, between 19 and 40 years of age, from leaving Paris. Our luggage was carefully examined, search being specially made for provisions and newspapers. It was quite a refreshment to one's eyes to see a tricolor flag at St.

Denis, not having seen anything but the red flag for three or four weeks. St. Denis was still occupied by Prussians, and each station on the line had its complement of German soldiers. Having been for five weeks without our boxes, which had been stopped at Boulogne, and, goods trains being suspended, there being no chance of getting them without going for them, I started the same day. The train from Chantilly stopped at Creil, and, having two hours to wait, I sauntered through the town. Like Chantilly, in addition to its being still occupied by Prussians, the town is filled with Paris people taking refuge from the perils of Paris. Creil used to be on our Paris plan, but the English workmen left at the outbreak of the war. As I stood upon the bridge, in the centre of which the tricolor was flapping in the breeze, and looked over the parapet upon the sluggish Oise rolling its yellow current under the arches, and heard mingling with the gurgling of the river the merry laugh of Prussian soldiers, who were smoking to their hearts' content close by, I thought of the last time I had stood upon that bridge in the midst of a knot of friends who are now scattered, northward to England, westward as far as Cobourg, Canada, and eastward as far as Lausanne. I strolled into the quaint old church. It was drawing towards evening, and the slantering rays of the westering sun, falling obliquely through the eastern stained-glass window upon the bizarre and medley architecture of the interior of the building, produced a most pleasing effect. The deep bass voice of a man came rolling along the arches to the extremity of the building, and was followed by the united shrill voices of children. I found that a priest was giving a Bible lesson. I planted myself behind a broad column where I could hear without being observed, and listened to one of the best Bible lessons I have ever heard. The doctrines of the Trinity in Unity, the Divinity and Proper Humanity of Christ, and the doctrine of redemption through the blood of Christ, were taught in a simple and beautiful manner. But, as is always the case in Roman Catholic churches, the pure doctrine was spoilt by the dragging in of Romish additions. The poor children were made at the close to join in a prayer to the Virgin Mary! I was reminded of the close of a splendid sermon I heard one week-evening in 1854 in the Cathedral of Avignon. The subject was the Judgment, and so powerful and faithful was the preaching that we were all brought in imagination before the great white throne. The like of it on that subject I have never heard. The priest concluded the sermon by an exhortation to the people to bring some flowers before the following Sunday to decorate the image of the Virgin!

When I got into the Boulogne train at Creil I found near me a very intelligent man, whose home is in Paris; so I proposed to him the following questions :—Why did the Government make the attack on Montmartre on the night of March 17 without being sure of success? Why did the Government leave Paris, and would they not by staying in Paris, have formed a nucleus around which the friends of order might have rallied and so quelled the rebellion? Why, when Admiral Saisset was sent from Versailles, did not the National Guards, said to be well affected, assemble in great numbers under the standard of order? How do you account for the great numbers of National Guards (far exceeding the opposite party) who desire order and peace, consenting to go out and fight the battles of the insurgents? Said a lady in our compartment, who, with her daughter, was flying from Paris, " *Voilà les cinq questions!*" All were eye and ear for the answer. The reply was, that the Government had treated the Montmartre affair with contempt, regarding it as a sort of bravado which they could any day put down when so disposed; that these insurgents were desperate fellows, who had nothing to lose, and held together, answering always to the *rappel*, whereas only three thousand friends of order assembled, the rest not caring to sacrifice their lives in what they supposed was an unequal contest, and, moreover, many of them not willing to fight for the Versailles government because of its law on the subject of the *échéances* (bills falling due); and that the men singly, unable to resist the march of three or four armed guards sent to force them to march, preferred to take the chance of battle to the risk of being shot out of hand.

My object accomplished, through the aid of the Rev. J. Gaskin, 1 returned at once to Chantilly, I had as fellow-passenger a Danish lady, whose home is in the Rue Malesherbes, and who was going to Paris to rescue, if possible, some of her plate from the hands of the brigands! a Frenchman, who thought that the Assembly at Versailles was very much to blame, and by its acts provoking instead of allaying civil war; a French lady, who has just placed her husband in safety at Amiens, and was herself returning to look after their affairs; and three Prussian officers, who were just returning from a six days' visit to England, and had been delighted with all they had seen, and especially with the Crystal Palace. My passport had been required and carefully scrutinised at Amiens on going to Boulogne; but at Longeau, on returning, the examination was painfully particular. "Where are you going? Who and what are you? What is the object of your journey?" Even this was not enough. A second official came in and took a seat in the carriage. "Your passport is all *en règle;* but what is your object in going towards Paris, and what are you;" "All well; but we must have proof of your identity. Have you any papers to show; I produced the printed card of our Methodist Chapel in the Rue Roquépine, Paris, with a list of the services. With this he was satisfied, and a smile came over his before stern face. "I beg your pardon, sir, but Monsieur Lyons (Lord Lyons) has begged us to be particular with English subjects." I was quite consoled for this strict examination by the thought that Lord Lyons was taking care to prevent the entrance into Paris of English vagabonds to fight the battles of the Commune.

Although at a distance of twenty-five miles, we hear the cannon distinctly at Chantilly. Last evening and this morning the canonnading has been continuous. We find a wide sphere of usefulness here. We hold English services for the English people, French services for the French people, and distribute tracts and speak to the German soldiers, who are here in great numbers.

Paris, May 3.

The situation of affairs in Paris remains much the same as when we were here a few days ago. Fort Issy has been all but taken, and on the Neuilly and Asnières side the Versailles troops have advanced, but there is no perceptible difference in the city—the same disposition on the part of the insurgents to fight on to the last, and the same sad and desolate aspect of the streets. In the Rue Royale I saw the great barricade, where the street joins the Place de la Concorde, which during the last few days has grown into a fortress. The barricade in our Boulevard, and almost close to our street, has not been proceeded with. The roadway of the line of the Boulevards is still comparatively empty. I could only see, as I stood at the end of the Boulevard de la Madeleine, an omnibus and two cabs in the whole length from the Madeleine to the corner of the Boulevard Montmartre. From the top of our tower I could distinctly hear the fusillading going on in the direction of Neuilly and Asnières. The cannonade, though not continuous, still rolled its dreadful boom through the city.

Among the many placards of the Commune upon the wall, I specially noted the following:—

"Sommation.

"In the name and by order of M. the Marshal (M'Mahon), Commander-in-Chief of the Army, we the major of the trenches, summon the commander of the insurgents, now in the Fort of Issy, to surrender himself and all the *personnel* shut up in the said fort. A delay of a quarter of an hour is allowed for a reply to this *Sommation*. If the commander of the insurgent forces declares, in writing, in his own name and that of the entire garrison of the Fort of Issy, that he submits, he and his, to this *Sommation*, with no other condition than obtaining life and liberty, with the sole exception of permission to reside in Paris, that favour will be granted. If no reply is sent in the course of the delay indicated, the whole garrison will be shot.

(Signed) "R. LEPERCHE.
"Tranchées before the Fort of Issy, April 30, 1871."

"Reply.

"To the Citizen Leperche, Major of the Trenches before the Fort of Issy.

"My dear Comrade,—The next time you send a *Sommation* so insolent as that contained in your yesterday's letter I shall have the man who brings it shot, according to the usages of war.—Your devoted comrade, (Signed) "ROSSEL,
"Délégué de la Commune de Paris."

A word as to this Rossel, who is well known to friends of ours. He is a Protestant, a member of Pastor Abric's church at Passy. He is quite a young man, not more than twenty-six, but a man of great energy and deep convictions. He has conscientiously embraced the cause of the Commune. He and Leperche were together at Metz, and were the principal leaders of the movement to oppose by force, shortly before the capitulation, the acts of Bazaine.

Our chapel at the Ternes has received another bomb in the staircase. Our Levallois chapel has been much injured. Two or three days ago a shell burst into the building, and, exploding, battered one of the walls, leaving the floor of the chapel covered with stones and plaster. I wait with trembling to hear of the fate of our chapel at Asnières.

May 7.

At our service this morning we had not a large congregation (fifteen in the morning, twenty in the evening), but God was with us both at the public service and the Sacrament of the Lord's Supper afterwards. All is quiet to-day; no sound of cannon. Not a single boom disturbed the quiet of our morning service. Before and during our evening service we heard occasionally the roll of cannon, but compared with former Sabbaths the day may be said to have been tranquil.

Monday Morning, May 8.

A notice is placarded on the walls announcing that the " Chapelle Expiatoire," close to us, is doomed to destruction, as being a standing insult to the spirit of revolution. Those who have visited Paris will well remember this little chapel, built over the place where the bones of Louis XVI. and Marie Antoinette were laid, and rested for twenty-two years, until their removal to St. Denis. Here also were buried the Swiss guards who lost their lives in defending the Tuileries. The two marble statues of Louis XVI. and Marie Antoinette in the little chapel are master-works of sculpture. Within eight days—so says the decree—this interesting memorial is to be levelled to the ground. This placard is signed by Rossel, Délégué à la Guerre, and dated *Floreal*, 79, the first official document of the Commune I have seen with the dates of the First Revolution. In passing near the Place Vendôme I observed a scaffolding around the base of the column, but of so slight a description that I cannot believe the insurgents are in earnest in their threat to pull it down. I had heard that straw manure was to be laid for it to fall upon. I see, however, no preparations of this kind. Let us hope also that the rumour of the threatened destruction of the statues of Henry IV. on the Pont Neuf, and of Louis XV. in the Place Royale, and other bronze statues, is a false report.

In addition to the great barricade at the end of the Rue Royale, I observe some stones and sand-bags laid across the street at the corner of the Rue St. Honoré. This, however, may not be the beginning of a new barricade, but an indication that carriages cannot enter that part of the Rue Royale. The stone barricades in and near the Place Vendôme have given place to larger and stronger barricades of earth and sand-bags, &c., at the entrance of the Rue Castiglione and at both entrances into the Rue St. Honoré. The barricade at the end of the Quai des Tuileries, adjoining the Place de la Concorde is assuming large proportions; and one of the most imposing of all is at the grand entrance of the Gardens of the Tuileries. One of the chief features of each barricade is a deep trench in front. The universal opinion is that the Commune will fight on to the end, and may hold out for several weeks longer. One is grieved to see in the battalions of the Commune some mere lads. I have observed lately boys of not more than fourteen or fifteen! Several placards announce increased facilities for the instruction of children, and also that schools are being established in which trades may be learnt. Many of these arrangements for the education of the people are admirable.

A red bill proclaims to Parisians that the Church of St. Nicolas des Champs has been opened for the meetings of a club, and exhorts citizens of other arrondissements to turn to a like useful purpose their parish churches. A young man, a member of our society, attended a meeting in St. Nicholas des Champs a few days ago. Men were smoking, drinking, and spitting on the floor. A rabid orator from the pulpit addressed the meeting in the wildest style, recalling the deeds of their grandfathers in 1793.

On Thursday last a meeting of Protestant pastors was held to decide as to whether any action should be taken by them as Protestant pastors in reference to some acts of the Commune, as, for example, that of the imprisonment of priests, &c. One was of opinion that the Communists were brigands, that no peace was possible with them, and that they must be driven away. Another, although milder in his view, was quite as much opposed to the Commune. Others thought there were points in which the Commune had the right on its side, and said they had members of their churches who conscientiously had espoused the cause of the Commune. The decision arrived at was to take no action at all.

There is talk of a *levée en masse*, a thing of course impossible. The Commune, however, is taking means to discover every Frenchman capable of bearing arms. A notice is placarded requiring all concierges, under heavy penalties, to furnish a list of all the persons in their houses, giving name, profession or business, place of birth, and age.

I think I see many signs of weakness in the Commune, and doubtless its days are numbered. The question now comes, what permanent effect upon the Government of France will have been produced by its existence for a few weeks in Paris? Some say that it will disgust people with the Republic, and make all France ready to receive a monarchy. Others think (and, as I believe, with more reason) that it is the Commune alone that has saved the Republic for

France, and that, even if it should soon cease to exist, the Commune will have secured a Republic for France at least for a few years, whatever may be the after course of events.

Paris, May 10, 1871.

The great event of to-day is the resignation of Rossel as *Délégué à la Guerre*. He was regarded by all as a man of talent and capacity, and his retirement is a great loss to the Commune. In his letter, addressed *aux citoyens membres de la Commune*, he states that either his orders have not been obeyed, or that they have been countermanded by others, and on such conditions he declines to hold the responsibility. He thus concludes his letter, "I retire, and have the honour of asking from you a cell at Mazas." Rochefort in the *Mot d'Ordre* agrees with Rossel in everything but his request for a cell at Mazas, and adds that in the present crisis the one thing to be done is to appoint a military dictator. Whether that dictator should be Rossel or another he leaves, but counsels that the Commune should choose its man without losing a single day. The Column Vendôme is still standing. Its fall is put off till Friday. Perhaps then it will be deferred till next Monday! Nor are there as yet preparations for the demolition of the *Chapelle Expiatoire*. The tricolour now floats on Fort Issy, and Fort Vanves is all but taken by the Government troops. The Commune is said to be almost dead, but it dies hard.

The sister of one of our French pastors, M. Dugand, successor to M. Jaulmes at the Rue Roquépine, has been imprisoned because her husband managed to escape from Paris. Pastor William Monod is interesting himself to secure her release, but so far has not succeeded. Our Ternes Chapel is escaping in a most wonderful manner. Beyond the slight injury caused by the two fragments which fell on the staircase, it has not suffered at all, although bombs have been falling on the right and the left. The other day a shell entered the house on one side, killed the wife of the concierge, and wounded the concierge himself. Another shell fell at the corner of the house on the other side, breaking a corner of the wall. In walking through *some* of the streets of the city, usually full of bustle and business, it seemed to me that I was walking through a city of the dead—no carriages on the roadway, no foot-passengers on the causeways, all silent and deserted, nothing to be heard but the echo of my footstep. The Boulevards, however, were a little more bustling than of late. Ugly dogs, with baskets in their mouths, soliciting alms for maimed or blind persons sitting alongside, fragments of bombs that had fallen in Paris offered for sale, and books, among which were many copies of the works of Voltaire, were to be seen on the broad asphalt. Shopkeepers were busy pasting strips of white paper, diamond-fashion, on their shop windows, with the idea of preventing the plate glass from being broken by the sudden shake that might be caused by the fall of the Vendôme Column, or by the explosion of gunpowder. There is a general impression that some parts of Paris will be blown up. From one of the numerous placards on the wall I learn that the Central Committee is again coming into power in military affairs. Its address to the people of Paris begins with the announcement in large characters that the Commune is sure of victory! The bombardment of the *enceinte* is still going on, but the cannonading is not so furious as for a day or two past.

May 11.

Passing along the Boulevards to-day, we saw from the end of the Rue de la Paix that ropes were fixed near the top of the *Colonne Vendôme*. This looks like an intention on the part of the Commune to carry out their threat to-morrow. I said to a man in a blouse near me, " Do they really mean to pull down the column?" " I don't know—pity if they do." " It is an historical monument; they can't destroy the history, if they destroy the monument." " No, let them take down the man at the top if they like, but the column ought not to be destroyed. Everybody who came to Paris went to see the *Colonne Vendôme;* if they go on destroying in this way there will soon be nothing left to see. What with the Versailles people and the Commune, Paris will soon not have a single monument to show. The Arc de Triomphe has been very much injured, and some of the bas-reliefs which cost so much labour and skill destroyed." Walking along our Boulevard Malesherbes, I saw a placard just posted up : " In its sitting of yesterday (seven o'clock in the evening) the Commune decided : 1. The nomination of citizen Delescluse to the functions of Délégué civil à la Guerre. 2. To send Colonel Rossel before the court-martial." Near it was another placard signed Delescluse, of which the following is a translation : To the Garde Nationale. Citizens, the Commune has delegated me to the Ministère de la Guerre : it has thought that its representative in the military administration ought to belong to the civil element. If I only consulted my own strength I should have declined this dangerous post, but I have reckoned on your patriotism to render the accomplishment more easy to me. The situation is grave, you know it ; the horrible war which the Federals, leagued with the remnants of the monarchical regimes, are making against you has already cost you enough generous blood ; nevertheless, while deploring these sad losses, when I behold the sublime future which will open for our children if it should not be given to us to reap what we have sown, I should salute again with enthusiasm the Revolution of March 18, which has opened to France and to Europe prospects which none of us dared hope for three months ago. To your ranks, then, citizens, and hold your ground before the enemy. Our ramparts are as solid as your arms and your hearts. You are not ignorant, besides, that you are fighting for your liberty and for social equality, that promise the fulfilment of which has so long escaped you ; that if your breasts are exposed to the balls and shells of the Versaillists, the prize which is assured to you is the freedom of France and of the world, the security of your hearths and the life of your wives and children. You will conquer, then: the world which contemplates you and applauds your magnanimous efforts is ready to celebrate your triumph, which shall be safety for all the people. *Vive la République Universelle! Vive la Commune!*"

Another notice placarded on the walls everywhere was to this effect: " The Committee of Public Safety decrees that the goods belonging to Thiers' property shall be seized, and the house of Thiers situated in the Place St. Georges razed to the ground." A long and wordy answer to the proclamation of M. Thiers is also placarded, and a larger bill than any of the rest announces another concert at the Tuileries for this evening at eight o'clock. Meetings of clubs are being held at many of the churches. Pastor Emile Cook was present at one of them, held at St. Eustache, and listened for some time to a torrent of nonsence and blasphemy. One speaker said there was no God, but that everything was *ideal*. Another that the religion of the Galilean was too old, but that the Galilean himself was in some respects excellent, always having remained a poor man and never having sought to get out of the ranks of the poor!

From the top of our tower we can see the bombardment of the forts and *enceinte*, which is now carried on with great vigour. Last evening a dense smoke covered Fort Vanves; and, if I may form a judgment at this distance, I should say that it is no longer tenable. The other forts on the south and south-east, Montrouge, Bicêtre, and Ivry, must soon fall into the hands of the Government. The general impression is that a grand attack on the city itself by the Versailles troops is imminent.

Summoned to-day to conduct a funeral service over the remains of an American banker (Mr. Richards, of the firm of Monroe and Co.), who died rather suddenly a few days ago, I had a fine opportunity of addressing a large company of Americans, who had assembled to sympathise with the bereaved family and show their respect for the memory of the deceased. May the seed sown on this solemn occasion spring up to the glory of God.

Our own services at Rue Roquépine are regularly attended by the few who remain in Paris, and in this time of trouble are truly times of refreshing. Our people, although some of them have been exposed to great danger, have all been kept from harm. Shells have exploded in the next apartment, or in the street within a few yards, but not one has been touched. So God keepeth his own.

May 14.

The Sabbath-day was ushered in with firing from the battery on the heights of Montmartre. This will inevitably, we fear, draw the fire of the Versailles troops further into the city. With the roar of cannon close at hand, we went down to our morning service; but, fortunately, during the time of service we had comparative quiet.

Throughout the day batteries have been sending their shells upon Vanves, Montrouge, &c., and upon the *enceinte*. The heavy boom was distinctly heard during our evening service, and two of our congregation who reside at Montmartre had to hasten home to place in safety their fragile things, lest they should be broken by the vibration from the cannon. The sun, which had been shining most brilliantly all day, sank over the west of the city in colour of deepest blood-red. Soon after the houses and monuments, shown out so beautifully in the clear evening light, had disappeared, the heavens towards the north-west were lighted up by the lurid glare of a fire. We found afterwards that it was a house set on fire by a shell.

Monday Morning, May 15.

Placards have not been posted so plentifully during the last day or two as in the earlier days of the Commune. Military announcements are, indeed, conspicuous by their absence. I observe, however, that Delescluse announces that the Federal troops have "swept Sablonville," and Grousset (Minister of the Commune for Foreign Affairs!) declares that the laws of the Geneva Convention have been scandalously disregarded by the assassins at Versailles, and wounded men have been summarily put to death, and tells that the Commune, influenced by civilisation, will still keep to the Geneva Convention, let the conduct of the assassins be what it may.

The Column Vendôme is still standing, but more ropes have been attached to the top, and the scaffolding enlarged at the base. A crowd of people in the Rue de la Paix were calmly contemplating the preparations. We went up to one of them and asked, "When is the Column to come down?" "I don't know, but I should think not before eight days." But they said it was to be pulled down on Friday, and then that this was the day on which it was to fall." "Yes, but it can't be taken down without making the proper preparations." "Well, I hope they won't take it down at all." "Ah, who knows but that the Versaillais will be in before they have a chance." The only one of the threatened demolitions really carried into effect as yet is that of M. Thiers' house in the Place St. Georges.

The barricade at the end of the Rue de Rivoli, in the Rue Castiglione and Rue St. Honoré, have been beautifully finished, and may be styled, in the barricade line, works of art. The muzzles of cannon stare out from the midst of the sandbags, and command the whole line of the streets. The barricade at the end of the Rue Royale will probably be the most imposing of all. As we passed it we saw six carts, laden with large bags filled with rags, making towards it to discharge their burden. All preparations are being made for a terrible resistance; for, although there is now an open feud between the Ministry of War, headed by Delescluse, and the Central Committee, which might end in a dissolution of the Commune, yet there are numbers of determined men, having nothing to lose, who will fight on to the last. The general opinion is that this affair cannot be ended without a fearful slaughter, nor without fighting from street to street and house to house. The temporary sheds erected in the gardens of the Tuileries have nearly all disappeared, and the gardens are assuming their old aspect.

Paris has never appeared to me cleaner and healthier than now. The city, except in the more open parts, has generally a sour smell, not perceptible by French people, but easily discernible by the keener olfactories of English people. Indeed, Paris, like Cologne, boasts of ninety-nine distinct odours. But, during the reign of the Commune, the city has been as sweet as any one could desire. I have accounted for it from the fact of more than one-third of the population having left, the ordinary operations for sweeping and cleansing the city being still carried on. It is strange to think of the Roman Catholic churches being used for their customary religious services in the morning, and for the meetings of clubs in the evening. An orator at one of the evening meetings boasted the other day of the superiority of this revolution in this particular, that the priests were willing to celebrate the mass, and allow secular meetings to be held in the churches at the same time, not considering the building desecrated by the secular evening meeting for the religious services in the morning.

We " assisted " at one of these meeting held at St. Eustache, which is regarded as the central meeting, delegates attending from all the clubs, and two or three members of the Central Committee being always present. The effect produced on my mind on entering the church was peculiar, and almost indefinable. I saw men walking in with their hats on; instinctively I took off my own. Passing by the aisles we managed to get near enough to the pulpit to hear very distinctly. The whole body of the church was crowded. Oh for such an audience to preach the gospel unto! Dim lamps surrounded the nave, the light just serving to make the darkness of the aisles visible. The lofty groined roof looked very beautiful in the hazy half-darkness. The orator, who had dared to invade the pulpit, spoke thus: " Have no pity on the assassins; they don't deserve any. The other day they bayoneted a poor wounded man on a litter." This remark caused a shudder of horror among the women near me. " We must demand the release of Blanqui. And if he be not released, the head of the Archbishop must fall." At this moment the assessor of the bureau (at all French meetings there is a *bureau*, consisting usually of chairman, vice-chairman, secretaries, and delegates) rose on the side of the nave opposite the pulpit, and said in a clear, strong voice, " I am glad you have touched on that subject. It was I who voted a few days ago for the death of the archbishop, and I call on you to vote it by acclamation." True, there were a few who shouted " *Oui, oui*," but to the honour of the meeting be it said that there was a very feeble response. We had heard enough, and left the meeting. A few days ago, at a meeting of *citoyennes* at St. Germain l'Auxerrois, a vote for a general divorce was carried by acclamation!

Paris, May 17, 1871.

The event of yesterday was the fall of the Column Vendôme; the event of to-day is a terrific explosion. At a quarter to six this evening every one was almost stunned, and the windows of our chapel were suddenly forced open. What could it be? As is usual, there were as many opinions as persons, but the general decision was, from the direction whence the terrible sound had seemed to come, that it was an explosion at Grenelle. The dense volume of smoke, seen from our tower, rising in that direction, confirmed the opinion. Our librarian and schoolmaster set off together to ascertain the truth. When they returned we learned that it was an explosion of the cartridge manufactory in the Avenue Rapp, that from a hundred to two hundred and fifty had been killed, and a great number wounded. Women were chiefly engaged in the manufacture of the cartridges, and they were the most numerous victims, but the National Guards on duty outside the manufactory, and some people who happened to be near at the time, are among the number of the dead. Many of the dead bodies were thrown by the violence of the explosion to the roofs of the neighbouring houses. Fragments of bodies and mangled limbs were to be seen in all directions.

The sight was most horrible to behold. The general idea throughout Paris is that this fearful event has been brought about by "malveilance," and that agents of Versailles have done it. Of this, however, there is no proof; indeed, everything that I hear confirms the belief that it was a pure accident. The only suspicious circumstance is that many women left the manufactory at five instead of six o'clock as usual. Fortunate that they did leave, or the loss of life would have been fearful. Four poor fellows have been arrested.

The long-looked-forwarded to, but often-deferred event—the fall of the Column Vendôme—took place yesterday. At three o'clock in the afternoon a *citoyen* mounted to the top of the column and shook the tricolour flag to indicate that the fall of the column would involve that of the flag. At half-past three the clarion sounded, the workmen came down from the scaffolding, the vast crowd was made to fall back, the *cabestan* (a machine for pulling the ropes) was set in motion. The column seemed to move. All eyes were fixed and anxious. But at this critical moment a heavy crack was heard. It was the *cabestan* breaking, and five or six workmen were thrown over, but not seriously hurt. A new apparatus was sent for, but it took at least two hours to bring and fix it. In the meantime some men worked with pickaxes, at the base of the column, and the bands of two or three battalions played martial and patriotic airs. Shortly before half-past five the new *cabestan* was set to work. The crowd was breathless.

The tension of the ropes made the column totter. An involuntary cry lest some terrible accident should occur, burst from every mouth, and was succeeded by a dead silence. After having oscillated for a moment, the mass of stone and bronze fell dislocated upon the bed of straw, manure, and branches prepared for it. An arm

of the statue was broken in the fall, and the head severed from the trunk. There was a great crackling of boughs, and clouds of dust rose into the air, but not the awful crash that had been expected. A tremendous clamour burst from the crowd, mingled with enthusiastic shouts of "Vive la Republique!" "Vive la Commune!"

To-day, in passing along the Boulevards, and looking along the Rue de la Paix, I could scarcely reconcile myself to the new look of the Place Vendôme, with the empty space instead of the beautiful column. Four red flags had been placed on the pedestal. The sight of the column celebrating the victories of the First Napoleon prostrate, and the statue of the Emperor lying dishonoured on the ground, awoke many reflections.

The Versailles troops are getting nearer and nearer, and the general impression is they will soon be within the ramparts.

Chantilly, Paris Circuit, May 20.

It being part of my ministerial duty to pay a friendly visit to Rheims once a year, I went on Thursday and returned yesterday. My route lay by Senlis and Soissons, and at both places every one in the train was obliged to show a passport. The news of Rochefort's arrest at Meaux on Friday last shows the reason of such minute examination. Soissons, the ancient and historical town on the edge of the forest Villers Cotterets, the burial-place of Kings Clothaire and Sigebert, is, it will be remembered, one of the towns that, during the late war, the commandant would blow up rather than yield; but after two days it capitulated! The bombardment of forty-eight hours, however, has left its mark on the town. The fortifications were much battered and a breach effected; the cathedral, which, though small, is one of the most beautiful in France, was struck in several places; and some shells broke through the two spire-crowned towers, the great ornaments of the town, and the only remains of the once magnificent Abbey of *St. Jean des Vignes.*

At Rheims I could almost have believed myself in a German town, so completely is it occupied by the invaders. The streets were filled with German soldiers; and in front of the colossal fabric, the pride of Rheims, where all the Kings of France were crowned, from the time of Phillippe Auguste to that of Charles X., with the exceptions of Henry IV. and Louis XVIII., Prussians with spiked helmets were listening, under the shadow of the far-famed portal of one of the grandest of French cathedrals, to the command to shoulder arms. I made my way to the house of the Rev. John Mearns, our minister at Rheims, and it being Ascension-day, a general holiday throughout France, went with him to a school treat he had prepared for the children of the day-school. About thirty bright and bonny English children sat down to tea and cake, and romped in downright English fashion in Mr. Holden's garden. I was the guest of Mr. Jonathan Holden, nephew of Mr. Isaac Holden, about whom and the arrangements of his factory a long article appeared in the *Standard* (afterwards copied into the *Watchman*) in September last. Mr. Holden went into Paris on urgent business, by the last train which entered the city before the investment by the Germans, and gave me the following account of his escape:—

"Finding myself, with our principal clerk, shut up in Paris, having had the misfortune to enter by the last train from Rouen on the night of the 17th September, to attend to important financial business, and feeling very strongly that my duty was at Rheims, among our suffering workpeople, who were exposed to all the rigours of the Prussians, of whose treatment I had already had some experience before leaving, I resolved at all hazards to make the attempt to cross the two belligerent lines, for which dangerous enterprise my journey through the Ardennes the week before, amid the terrible scenes of the late battles and their concomitant evils and misery had partly prepared me; but, before desperately running the gauntlet, I adopted all possible means to get through under shelter of an escort or flag of truce. I went first to our Embassy, and saw the only remaining attaché; he said he was powerless to render the least service, nevertheless was well disposed to make an effort, and fixed an hour in the afternoon for me to call again. Not to lose precious time I made an effort myself with General Trochu, but failed to get further than the ante-chamber. I then called upon Mr. Rouland, the Governor of the Bank, who kindly gave me a letter of introduction to the General, begging him to aid by any means in his power my departure. I was at once admitted, and found him overwhelmed with most urgent despatches from all the forts around Paris. He at once ordered us a special *sauf conduit* to enable us to pass freely through their lines, but could not do more, adding that it was rash to make the attempt to leave the city. I then returned to the Embassy, and the attaché told me that he could not aid me in any way, not even to procure me a pass. I told him that I had succeeded in getting a *sauf conduit*, but now requested advice as to how to pass into the Prussian Camp. He said, you have already procured what I have failed in, and in the rest will be more successful, as I cannot see M. Jules Favre at present (he had left Paris for the Prussian head quarters). I then went to the river, but failed; afterwards to Charenton, but was not allowed to pass, as a severe combat was going on in that direction, especially around Villejuif. We then drove to St. Denis, and arrived there in time to get into the heat of a contest going on to the right of the *Double Couronne*, towards Stains, from which wounded were being brought back to the city. We were therefore obliged to return, over innumerable difficulties, to Paris. It was Tuesday night, the 20th September. I saw a good number of friends, but all advised me to stay; nor would they aid me in any way. Nevertheless I agreed with the cabman who had driven us to St. Denis, to take us out next morning by a special route which he knew well, for which we agreed to pay him 4,000f. down, and 3,000f. if any accident occurred to his horses or cab, but he never made his appearance. I again saw our military attaché at the British Embassy, who tried to dissuade us from making the attempt, as he saw no possibility of our getting through. I then called upon M. Jules Simon, who gave me a note to M. de Keratry (the Prefect) as the person most likely to be of service to us. When I saw him he said, " Your case has already been before me three times by friends whom I should be most happy to serve, but really I cannot; neither will I take the responsibility to even advise." I replied that I was fully resolved to leave ; and the only favour that I would now ask was that he would inform me where the least fighting was going on, and at the same time where I should meet the greatest body of Prussians, as I was not wishful to fall in with a few straggling troops without officers. He said, "At this moment in the direction of Romanville ; but I will not undertake to say what will be the case even there an hour hence. My determination was taken at once. Accompanied by my French friend I took a cab and drove to Messrs. Rothschilds tô deposit the principal part of our mouey for a cheque upon London. They most kindly rendered the service, though money just then in Paris was a charge and extra risk, and not at all useful. We also deposited our luggage with a friend, and made for the barrier of Romainville, where we were allowed to pass on foot to the Fort. We were received very courteously by the Commandant. After hearing our request, he advised us strongly not to venture, assuring us that we could never pass his lines, and saying, " My men will not regard your pass ; they may bring you before me several times, that is, if they will take the trouble ; but I will again release you. I cannot prevent you making the effort with your *sauf conduit*, but will not aid you in the least." As a favour I requested him to give orders to his men not to fire upon us from the Fort: he said, "I cannot, nor will I leave my room to assist you." We left him in this mood and quitted the Fort, which was vomiting forth its shells into the woods behind Bondy, or wheresoever the spiked helmet was to be seen. We took to our right, and immediately turned down the road leading to Noisy-le-Sec. When scaling the breastwork at its head, we were accosted by a sentinel who allowed us to pass, and pointed out an easier by-path. We followed his direction. On entering this by-path my companion exclaimed, 'Are you really going?' I said, 'Yes, but you may remain, and can make yourself useful in Paris;' he replied, 'No, if you leave I will not allow you to go alone, but will follow.' I soon discovered that we should be exposed to stray shots, and perhaps be a mark for the *franc tireurs*, if we continued among the bushes and fields: we therefore made for the main road, which was encumbered with the fine large trees that had a short time before formed a pleasant avenue. We climbed over tree after tree, always remaining in the centre of the road. The *franc tireurs* were as thick as the trees and bushes permitted. I induced one of them to accompany us for some distance towards Noisy-le-Sec. Before entering the village we were gruffly accosted by a *franc tireur* who had had part of his képi shot away that morning. I recognised and went at once up to him saying, 'I know that face; are you not from Rheims?' he said, 'I am, and worked there at ——.' Well, you should know me, I am ———.' 'Of course I know you; what are you doing out here amid so much danger?' 'I am going to Rheims.' 'What can I do for you? come to my commandant,' and at once he conducted us to him. The commandant received us most sternly; but, when he leant that we were from Rheims, he changed his tone and began to enquire most kindly about several dear friends, charging me to give them news of him if we should ever arrive. He told us that we had before us a most perilous journey, but added, 'I will conduct you to our *avant poste*, and would gladly go with you to the Prussian out-post if those gentlemen were conducting the war upon human principles.' We asked him how long we should have to walk before coming in sight of the Prussians. 'About one hour and a half,' he said. On arriving at the extreme limit we jumped over the barricade, and our kind conductor exclaimed, with a graceful wave of the hand, '*à la grace de Dieu!*' 'Twas a most solemn hour and a half, never, indeed, to be forgotten. We passed through Bondy most of which was in flames, without encountering any living creature save a few dogs and cats that still clung to the deserted village. On all that beautiful landscape hung dark clouds of smoke arising from the country residences and homesteads. Shortly after leaving Bondy, we discovered the glistening bayonets and casques of the Prussians, for it was a bright clear day. I said to my friend, 'If they fire we may both fall, and they may then come to fetch us.' At the same time I wrapped my overcoat round my arm and laid it across my breast. As we neared came the welcome sound 'Halt!' as none but a German can utter it. They motioned to us to advance, and again to halt; and thus we were allowed to pass the first outpost. The men were placed along the bank of the canal, and behind the trees lining the road, and were lying down in the ditches with their muskets pointed towards us by the score. Once allowed to meet, however, I felt quite safe. Then I remembered that I had eaten nothing that day, and little for a day or two before. I requested to be allowed to sit down, and asked for a little bread if possible; but they said that they had not received any rations that day. We remained there about an hour, and then moved to another part of the wood, and then another, and thus moved about, but always under shelter of the wood. In moving from the first rendezvous, they pointed out a terrible hole made by a bomb in the road close by where they all had a narrow escape but a few minutes before; the shells were constantly falling at random among the trees of Raincy. About six we went with the main body to Clichy. On our way an officer with whom I was walking pointed out a man in a blouse whom they were conducting into the fields to shoot as a spy; and on entering Clichy the soldiers off duty remarked, as we passed, "there go two others to be shot. The officer growled at them in anything but an agreeable tone. On our arrival our papers were demanded, and during their examination, our guard, who appeared to take great interest in our position, said, 'I am a soldier, but would not attempt to accomplish what you have done to-day, nor even now should I like to be in your position.' I replied 'We are now all safe, only hungry. Can you procure some bread for us?' He went into the room where were the officers examining our papers one of whom immediately brought us a large piece of bread and two glasses of wine, for which we were very thankful. Never did I find bread so sweet. Our papers were made out for Belgium at the German head-quarters of Rheims, though they were aware that our mission was to Paris; but, not being in possession of the road, they gave a *sauf conduit* for Belgium, therefore I was requested to give a reason for being in Paris, &c. Finally, I requested to be sent to the Royal head-quarters, as it was Count Moltke himself who made out our papers. The officials at Clichy were exceedingly kind and gentlemanly, and decided to send us at once, with an escort, to Coubron, the head-quarters of the Saxon troops, where we arrived at a late hour, and then went through another severe examination of much the same kind. After conferring together, the General said with great emphasis, 'And you have come out of Paris to-day?' 'Yes, at noon.' 'You have come out of Paris?' 'Well, my men have not executed my orders, which were to allow no one to leave; it is, indeed a miracle that you are here, and I am only sorry that I cannot accommodate you for the night, as you must remain with me.' He added, pointing to a mattress, 'That is all I have for myself.' He sent us into an empty room; but soon chairs, and also bread, meat, and wine, were brought, at last two mattresses. My friend was sad indeed; and when pressed to lie down, he replied, 'I would gladly, if it were my bed of death.' After a while the General came to our room to learn something of Paris, and asked if there was still something to eat, &c. We pleaded ignorance, having been only a few days there. He most generously said on leaving, 'I see you are not wishful to say anything, and you are perfectly right; I admire your caution, good night.' In the morning he sent us coffee and bread; but I could not prevail on my friend to take any refreshment. He added, 'I would if it were poison.' Come, come, you are perfectly safe now; what makes you so sad?' He replied, 'It is your cheerfulness that makes me sad; you had no occasion to leave Paris.' I said, 'I had no duty in Paris, and should have been an extra mouth and a burden to them. My clear duty lay at Rheims, and since the decision was taken I have had no fear, but should have ever despised myself if I had remained.' He said, 'Well, you are right; but it is death to me to see my poor country thus overrun by an exacting enemy.' We were kept long into the day, but finally sent forward to Claye with an escort; the General expressing his regret at not being able to procure a carriage for us, but said, 'I have given instructions that they procure one for you at Claye.' Then we were safely delivered over to the commandant, who was kind and considerate, and gave us wine, bread, and raw bacon, which latter was a great boon throughout the war to the German army. We did not remain long. The commandant told us that we had now our liberty, and was sorry that he could not provide a conveyance for us, but said, ' I have given you a written authority to stop any military carriage and mount.' We then started off on foot for Meaux, under a burning sun. The country was indeed lovely, with all the late crops still on the ground, and all the vines laden with their abundant and luxuriant charge, but not one solitary inhabitant did we meet between Paris and Meaux. All the villages quite deserted, nothing but military trains, and movements of troops, as if all Germany were pouring into poor France. When nearing Meaux we found a way-side inn, and hoped to get some little refreshment; but the moment we presented ourselves the poor woman nearly lost her senses, and began to beg us to kill her at once. Nothing, however, could we procure. There followed us a most brutish gang of camp followers whose conduct was such that I did not wonder at the state of the poor woman. All these ruffians wore the *brassard* of the Geneva Convention. Such were the only people we met in our walk of forty kilometers. We passed the night at Meaux, and next morning saw the commandant to get his visa. We happened to meet a Queen's messenger returning to Berlin, who kindly gave us places forward to Epernay. We stayed one night at Dormons, and arrived at Rheims on Saturday night the 24th of September, after a fortnight's perils and adventures, and found my house still occupied as Prussian barracks, and the town crowded with Prussian soldiers."

I learnt from several reliable persons at Rheims, in reference to the German occupation, that the excellent character given in some English newspapers, as for example, the *Times* and *Daily News*, to the Germans, and especially to the German officers, for their consideration and gentlemanly conduct, is by no means deserved. The universal testimony is that during the first fortnight of the occupation a tide of lawless plunder swept over the country. The general opinion, however, is that, much as may be said against the Germans in France, the French would have been far worse if they had succeeded in entering Germany.

Paris, May 21.

Before the dawn of this day of rest began a terrible battle just outside the fortifications, which lasted till six o'clock. The night before there had been fighting along the whole line from eleven p.m. till four a.m. The result has been hundreds, if not thousands, of dead and wounded, a universal discouragement among the insurgents, and an expectation that within a short time the Versaillais will be within the gates of the city. During our morning service there seemed to be some relaxation in the cannonading, for we did not hear a single rumble of cannon or mitrailleuse during the whole time. It was a quiet and blessed season—one to be remembered—though our number was only fifteen! Some who could not come to the service called on us in the afternoon. The first was a man from Asnières, who had come to tell me that his wife, a regular attendant at our Asnières chapel, had been killed by a shell. The poor fellow burst into floods of tears while giving me the following sorrowful recital. The cannonading had become so heavy around his dwelling that he had fitted up the cellar for his wife and four children to live in, and had told them to go down to this place in safety. The four children he had taken down himself, and begged his wife to go, but she lingered to cook some meat for their dinner. While she was leaning over the frying-pan a shell from a *wagon blindé* on the railway belonging to the Commune had entered the cottage, and burst close to the poor woman. Seven fragments struck her, laying her flat on the ground, and scattering above and around her in hopeless confusion beds, bedding, tables, and chairs. Her husband, employed at a factory close by, hearing the noise, rushed to the house, and called his wife by her name. No response. A second call, "Where are you, Polly?" The voice of his youngest child answered from a corner of the room, "Mother's up there." The child had stolen up from the cellar, and was in the room when the bomb exploded, but was not hurt! "Children, where are you?" Three voices from the cellar replied, "We're all here, father." Removing chairs, tables, and bedding, the husband saw stretched on the floor the lifeless body of his wife. The three children had in a moment been made motherless, and himself a widower. A second member of my congregation came just as this poor man went out. She had not been able to attend the morning service; had been aroused at three o'clock by the terrific fusillade, which, although she was not living far from the centre of the city, in the Rue de la Victoire, seemed so near that she could scarcely believe that the Versailles troops were not within the city. A member of my class came next to tell me she could not come to the service because of the presence, in the house of which she was concierge, of some people whose absence would be much more agreeable to her. The house was next to the Mairie of the Eighth Arrondissement, and under pretence that the windows overlooked the courtyard of the Mairie, and that the National Guards might be shot by any one posted there, they decided that the house must be occupied. Accordingly an insurgent commandant had established himself in the apartment of the first floor, and *factionaires* (armed men) kept guard at the door. She had been faithful in speaking boldly to the commandant, who professed not to believe in God and religion, and was not without hope that some impression had been produced on his mind. Her account of the origin of this man and his surroundings were some answer to the question constantly asked as to these soldiers of the Commune, "*D'où cela sort-il?*" This commandant, now occupying with his family a grand apartment on the first floor in the Rue d'Anjou St. Honoré, was a riding master at the Hippodrome, and his aide-de-camp was a stable boy! The valorous commandant had kept a carriage at the door of the house throughout Friday night all ready to convey him safely away in case the need had arisen.

The Rev. Emile Cook next came in, and told us that a second meeting of Protestant pastors had been held, and a written request to the members of the Commune to release the Archbishop of Paris and other priests had been signed by twenty-two Protestant pastors and laymen, and was to be presented by a deputation from their number; that Pastor E. de Pressensé had attended a *séance* of the *jury d'accusation*, presided over by Raoul Rigault, to decide which among the prisoners should be retained as hostages, and had witnessed a mockery of justice such as one reads of in connection with the First Revolution; and that the Commune had published a law forbidding prostitution, and condemning all that were proved guilty of robbery to the penalty of death.

Our evening service was greatly disturbed by the roll of cannon. The white lines of smoke on the hills on the south side of the city, as seen from the top of our tower, and the whizzing of shells from Mont Valérien, indicate the continuance of the bombardment; and at nine o'clock this evening the quickly succeeding flashes in the direction of Passy and Auteuil denote the beginning of a fusillade, perhaps of the general attack!

Chantilly, Paris Circuit, May 23, 1871.

We got out of Paris just before the city was isolated, the communications interrupted, and the gates closed. The Northern line was cut about two hours after our train passed. We heard in Paris on Sunday afternoon that the Versailles troops had entered the city, but we could scarcely believe it. We found, however, the following morning that the news was true; at least that some troops under Commandant Trèves passed the St. Cloud Gate at half-past three on Sunday afternoon, although the great bulk of the army did not enter till Monday morning. A telegram from the Government of Versailles was posted at the Chantilly Station yesterday (Monday) morning: " Versailles, 4.30 a.m. A part of the army is already in Paris. We have the gates of St. Cloud, Passy, and Auteuil. We are masters of the Trocadero." This (Tuesday) evening I have seen some one just returned from St. Denis, who brings the news that a telegram of the Government was posted this afternoon, and dated, " Versailles, May 23, 2 p.m.," announcing that the troops were in possession of the Tuileries and the Louvre, and had surrounded Montmartre. Another telegram at 4.30 p.m. had announced that Montmartre is taken. All yesterday we heard the cannon very distinctly; it was heard all through the night; and this morning it was more furious than ever, accompanied by detonations which sounded like explosions, and not the ordinary roar of the cannon; but this evening, thank God, all is still. May the horrid sound never be heard more! Now that this sad civil strife is nearing its close, my memory brings before me the appearance of the city during the last hours of the Commune. Passing along the Rue Neuve des Capucines, which is in a line with our Rue Roquépine, I observed that the iron chains surrounding the *Chapelle Expiatoire* had been removed, and some of the stones displaced, the beginning of the demolition of the monument. Happily the destruction of this historical building has been prevented by the entrance of the troops. I wish they had been in a week earlier, so as to have prevented the fall of the *Colonne Vendôme*. Sad indeed was the sight of that prostrate column as we saw it the other day. We had made our way through the fortress-barricade at the end of the Rue Royale, a compact wall of sand-bags rising to a great height on each side of the narrow passage; and then, crossing the Place de la Concorde, through the barricade at the end of the Rue de Rivoli. Both these barricades were strengthened with stone work, with regular steps leading from the lower to the higher parts of the fortification. We proceeded along the Rue de Rivoli, and turned up the Rue Castiglione, the view along the Rue de la Paix seeming strange without the column. At last, nearing the barricade, we took to the Arcade on the left, but soon found a bayonet in front of us, and the smiling face of a National Guard beckoning us to the other side of the street, as the *sortie* was there. In single file we passed close to the houses, the huge barricade filling up the greater part of the arcade. Learning that by a *détour* we could get into the centre of the Place Vendôme, we went along the Rue St. Honoré, Rue Marché St. Honoré into the very middle of the Place, and stood beside the fallen monument. Some men were at work with pickaxes, upon the top of the pedestal, apparently levelling the stonework still remaining at the base of the column. From the near view we gained of the prostrate mass of stone and bronze, we found that the covering of bronze was very thin. Most of it had been stripped from the stone, and was lying in heaps at the side, but about the middle of the column there was a portion remaining intact in its spiral coil around the stone. We thus gained a good view of a part of the historical bas-relief, which before we had seen only at a distance. The chief point of interest, however, was the colossal bronze statue. There was the figure of the great, talented, ambitious, unscrupulous man in the Roman costume, lying flat on the ground in the very centre of the city in which he was once almost worshipped. A feeling came over me exactly like that which I experienced when I stood, in the midst of shapeless ruins of Memphis, beside the one great prostrate statue, possibly that of the great Rameses. In Paris, Napoleon I., once the idol of the Parisians, finds no one to speak well of him. "None now so base as do him reverence." The shopkeepers near the Place Vendôme (for the fall of the column was, during a day or two, the one subject of conversation) join in saying, "Ah! France owes all her misfortunes to him and his nephew." Such is the instability of human glory! In the general view of Paris from the top of our tower I quite miss the statue. There it used to be, overtopping the neighbouring houses, apparently close to the Madeleine. I was accustomed of late constantly to look in that direction to assure myself that the column was still standing; but now there is only an open space!

On Sunday afternoon last Paris seemed to be *en fête*. There have never been such crowds in and around the Place de la Concorde except on some extraordinary occasion, such as the fête of the 15th August under Imperialist rule, and everyone appeared to be in holiday dress. At that very time the Versailles troops were in Paris! Never has a city been more completely kept under and cowed than Paris during the last two months under the rule of the Commune. No one dared to utter a word against the Commune lest a bird of the air should carry the voice. The reply to the question, "What think you of the present state of affairs?" was "*On n'ose que penser.*" "One dare only think." The press was completely gagged. Newspapers were successively suppressed until not one was left but such as expressed the wishes of the Commune. A medical man, in a hired cab on his way to a post of great danger to care for the wounded, when, a shell having exploded near, the cabman refused to proceed, had only to put his head out of the window and say. "*Vous êtes réquisitioné par la Commune,*" and the cab bounded along at a pace never attained in ordinary times under the utmost possible pressure.

May 24.

We have seen from St. Denis this day a sight such as we shall never forget. Fires have been seen in various parts of the city throughout the whole day; but in the evening, towards nine o'clock, the heavens in the direction of the ill-fated city were completely lighted up. If we had not during the last sad few weeks seen how little comparative damage has been done by what has appeared to be a tremendous conflagration, we should have thought all Paris was on fire. We climbed to the fifth story of a house near the canal-bridge, and thence gained as good a view as it was possible to obtain. From this point of observation we distinctly saw (1) a terrible fire at La Chapelle, (2) a mass of flame between La Chapelle and Montmartre, which seemed to be either at La Villette or in the interior of the city in the direction of the Tuileries and the Hôtel de Ville (3) a smouldering fire on the right of Montmartre, apparently in the direction of Vaugirard. The heavy roll of cannon broke on our ear as we looked on the fearful sight. No one could tell exactly from what part of the city the sound came, but it was generally supposed that it was the battery of the Buttes Chaumont, the last stronghold of the insurgents, firing on Montmartre, which is now occupied by the Government troops. Montmartre rose dark and black in the midst of the surrounding fires, and immediately behind Montmartre all was dark, betokening that the quarter of the Madeleine was safe: so we have no fear for our Rue Roquépine Chapel, unless from the

Buttes Chaumont the insurgents should carry out, by sending some shells into the midst of it, their vow of vengeance often expressed against the Eighth Arrondissement (in which our chapel is situate) because most of the National Guards fled after the outbreak of the insurrection.

As we gazed upon the burning city and the lurid glare of the sky, we could not but recall some passages in the 18th chapter of the Book of the Revelation : " Alas ! alas ! that great city that was clothed in fine linen and purple and scarlet, and decked with gold, and precious stones, and pearls !" " and cried when they saw the smoke of her burning, saying, What city is like unto this great city !"

We met a man who showed us some charred pieces of paper which he had picked up at Houille, twelve miles from Paris, about one o'clock, the time when a terrible explosion was heard, supposed to be the blowing up of the Hôtel de Ville. On these blackened shreds could be made out words in writing, showing that they were " actes de naissance," probably from some mairie or from the Hôtel de Ville.

As we returned by train to Chantilly, we could see the fire distinctly for a distance of at least ten miles. On a bridge over the railway near Gonesse a crowd of people " stood afar off " looking towards Paris, " and lo, the smoke thereof went up as the smoke of a furnace."

May 26.

This evening we went to St. Denis to ascertain as much as possible, by personal observation, the course of events. Soon after the train emerged from the Chantilly forest, we saw a bright light in the sky, betokening the continuance of fires in the city. As we drew nearer the light brightened until we could see, at a distance of at least twelve or fourteen miles from Paris, a brilliant flame. Various points in the horizon towards the south were lighted up as from smouldering fires, and the whole length of the city was covered with smoke. The flame increased in intensity as we neared St. Denis. We counted four great fires, but could not make out exactly where they were. One of them was much larger than the rest, the flames rising to a great height and covering the clouded heavens throughout half their expanse with a crimson hue. How little did we dream when walking through the beautiful streets on Sunday last of the extent of the calamity that was about to befal the city! On our return we did not lose sight, except while passing through the forest, of the glare of the fires, and even when we reached the Chantilly station we could still see the sky completely lighted up in the direction of Paris. A notice was posted at the Mairie here yesterday, asking, on behalf of the Government, for young men *de bonne volonté* to serve as firemen, and go up to Paris with fire engines. Twelve men dressed as firemen, with all the necessary equipment, left Chantilly yesterday afternoon. In the evening numbers of *pompiers* from Beauvais, Amiens, and other towns passed the Chantilly station on their way to the burning city.

The three official despatches of the Government sent to all the authorities, civil and military, throughout France during this week have been :—

" Versailles, May 23, 4.30 a.m.

(1) " Half the army is already in Paris. We have the gates of St. Cloud, Passy, and Auteuil. We are masters of the Trocadero."

Versailles, May 23, 2.10 p.m.

(2) " Events follow the course we had a right to hope for. There are ninety thousand men in Paris. The General Cissey is established at the Mont Parnasse Railway Station, at the Ecole Militaire, and has followed the left bank of the Seine as far as the Tuileries. The Generals Douay and Vinoy are surrounding the Tuileries, the Louvre, the Place Vendôme, to advance afterwards to the Hôtel de Ville. General Clinchant, master of the Opera, the St. Lazare Railway Station, and Batignolles, has just carried the barricade of Clichy. He is also at the foot of Montmartre, which General Ladmirault has turned with two divisions. General Montaudon, following outside the movement of General Ladmirault, has taken Neuilly, Levallois Perret, Clichy, and is attacking St. Ouen. He has taken 105 cannon and mitrailleuses ; and everything leads to the hope that if the struggle does not terminate to-day, it will be finished tomorrow, and for a long time. The number of prisoners amounts already to five or six thousand ; it will be doubled to-morrow. As to the number of killed and wounded insurgents, it is

impossible to speak certainly, but it is considerable. On the side of our army the losses have been small."

Montmartre was taken about the time the above despatch was written.

"Versailles, May 25, 7 am.

(3) "We are masters of Paris, except a very small portion, which will be occupied this morning. The Tuileries are in ashes; the Louvre is saved; the part of the Ministère des Finances which abuts on the Rue de Rivoli is burnt. The Palace Quai d'Orsay, in which sat the Council of State and Cour des Comptes, has been also burnt. Such is the state of Paris. Twelve thousand prisoners; we reckon that we shall have eighteen to twenty thousand. The ground is strewn with dead bodies. The frightful spectacle will serve as a lesson, it is to be hoped, to the foolish people who dared to declare themselves partisans of the Commune. Justice will soon receive satisfaction. The human conscience is indignant at the monstrous deeds of which France and the whole world have just been witnesses. The conduct of the army has been admirable. We are happy, in the midst of our misfortunes, to be able to announce that, thanks to the wisdom of our generals, our loss is but small."

May 27, 7 p.m.

We have just received a letter, *posted in Paris*, from Mr. Chastel, our librarian at Roquépine, the first letter from Paris the Chantilly postman has delivered for two months. He tells us that he is well, and that the whole house has been safely kept. Some rifle balls entered the building, but no one was wounded. He adds : " Paris is quite devastated—a considerable portion burnt. The insurrection is conquered, but what a mass of ruins it has left! No one can go out of

Façade des Tuileries.

Paris. God has mercifully kept me from all danger, but many have fallen. You will learn with sorrow that Madame Paris and her brother (the Madame Paris who, with her husband, has carried on so successful a work of evangelisation among the *chiffoniers*) were struck by a ball in their room on Tuesday morning. They were buried last evening (Thursday) at six o'clock. The Rue Royale, the Tuileries, Hôtel de Ville, Cour des Comptes, Légion d'Honneur, Grenier d'Abondance, some churches, barracks, &c., &c., have been burnt by the insurgents, and are completely destroyed. *Frightful! frightful!* But that which oppresses me the most is the

Hôtel de Ville.

thought of the thousands of lives sacrificed, the souls that have passed into eternity without any preparation. Oh! my heart bleeds! Among all our friends and acquaintances I hear of none killed except the two whom I have mentioned. I have passed a good night for the first time since Saturday. I do not hear the cannon, but know not whether all the quarters are conquered. There are fires in all directions. Women and children are going about in all the quarters, and pouring petroleum through all the air-holes of the cellars and underground storehouses. Everybody is taking the precaution of having them stopped up."

In the *Paris Journal* of to-day we find the following sad account of the fires in Paris :—

Les Tuileries, absolutely consumed except the thick walls. *Le Louvre*, saved, except the library. *Le Palais de Justice*, a ruin. *Le Palais Royal* all the part formerly inhabited by the Prince Napoleon destroyed, the neighbouring houses preserved. *Le Châtelet*, burning still. *Les Arts et Métiers*, consumed. *Le Grenier d'Abondance*, nothing but enormous smoking *débris*. *L'Hôtel de Ville*, with its archives, documents, library, and history of Paris, a ruin ; *L'Eglise St. Eustache*, the beginning of a fire produced by a petroleum-bomb, which was soon extinguished. The clock-tower partially destroyed by shells, but the main part of the church saved. *Le Légion d'Honneur*, in ashes. *Le Conseil d'Etat, la Cour des Comtes*, in ashes. *Le Ministère des Finances*, partly burnt. *Le Port St. Martin*, burnt. *L'Entrepôt*, in flames. *Les Gobelins*, destroyed." Some of these buildings were scarcely injured ; but this is the list as it appeared in the *Paris Journal*.

Such is the mournful list ; and we learn that women, more like furies than human beings, have taken a fiendish part in the work of destruction. They have, however, done their worst, the remaining insurgents being now pursued to their last stronghold, Belleville, whence doubtless they will soon be dislodged. Notwithstanding this fearful destruction, anyone who takes in his hand a map of Paris and compares what has been destroyed with what remains, will see but little of the city has been devastated. The finest monuments, the Madeleine, Notre Dame, the Sante Chapelle, the Church of the Invalides, the Arc de Triomphe, &c., &c., still remain, and I venture to predict that, although I have no hope that the city will be rebuilt in a year, in twenty years from this time Paris will be more magnificent than ever. Some verses in Revelation xviii., it is true, have wonderfully described the present doleful condition of the city, but I have no belief that the prophecy of the chapter refers to Paris. There are some verses which lead to the supposition that it refers with far greater probability to such a city as London !

May 28.

I have just received a letter from one of our local preachers who is taking the services to-day at Rue Roquépine, as it is impossible for me to get in. I am preaching at the chapel here at Chantilly. Here is the letter :—

" Paris, Thursday Morning.

" We have passed through a terrible season, but have been preserved. We are all safe and well at the chapel. I am writing on the top of a drum near Montmartre, having followed the troops to attend to the wounded. I have just witnessed the execution of twenty-five women who were found pouring boiling water upon the heads of the soldiers. A great portion of the city is in flames."

May 20.

The two following official Government despatches have been posted at the Mairie yesterday and to-day :—

May 27, 11.40 a.m.

"The troops have conquered all the forts, carried the Place de la Bastille, the Château d'Eau, the Prince Eugène Barracks, the railway stations, and now there is nothing left but to occupy Belleville. We have made more than 20,000 prisoners."

May 28, 9.30 p.m.

" Our *corps d'armée*, charged to operate upon the right bank, was yesterday evening ranged in a circle at the foot of the Buttes Chaumont and the heights of Belleville. This night they have surmounted all obstacles. General Ladmirault has passed the *Bassin de la Villette*, the Cattle Market, and ascended the Buttes Chaumont and the heights of Belleville. Young Drouot, so worthy of the name he bears, carried the barricades, and this day Ladmirault's corps crowned the heights. On his side Douay's corps left the Boulevard Richard Lenoir in order to reach the same positions of Belleville. At the same time General Vinoy mounted the Cemetery of Père Lachaise, carried the Mairie of the Twentieth Arrondissement and the prison of la Roquette.

The sailors showed everywhere their accustomed *entrain*. Entering la Roquette we had the consolation of saving 269 hostages who were about to be shot; but alas! the wretches from whom we are obliged to snatch Paris burnt and bloody, had had the time to shoot seventy-four of them, among whom, we have the sorrow of announcing, are the Archbishop of Paris, the Abbé Deguerry, curé of the Madeleine (the best of men), the president Bonjean, and many men of merit and of rare and excellent qualities. After having put to death, during these last days, the generous Chaudey, a man full of heart and goodness, and an inveterate republican, whom could one hope they would spare? Now, driven back to the extremity of the *enceinte* between the French army and the Prussians, who refuse to let them pass, they are about to expiate their crimes, and have nothing more to do but either to die or give themselves up. The too culpable Delescluze was picked up dead by the troops of General Clinchant. Millière, not less famous, has been shot for having fired a revolver three times at a corporal who arrested him. These expiations do not atone for so much misery, for so many crimes; but they ought to teach these mad people that men do not provoke and set civilization at defiance in vain; and that soon justice makes itself heard and felt. The insurrection, shut up within the space of some few hundred yards, is conquered, definitely conquered. Peace is about to spring up again, but it will not be able to chase from honest and patriotic hearts the profound grief with which they are penetrated."

May 29, 6 p.m.

☞ The *Paris Journal* has just arrived, announcing that " the army of order is now completely mistress of Paris." Among the items of news we learn, in contradiction of the former report, that the Odeon and Châtelet are not burnt; that the great fire we saw from St. Denis on Friday night was at the great storehouses near the docks at Villette.

Chantilly, Paris Circuit, May 31, 1871.

We have received two letters from Mr. Chastel, our librarian at the Rue Roquépine, which have reached us by the regular post, showing that postal communications are now re-established. From these letters I translate the following extracts:—

Paris, May 22.

Since eight o'clock this morning there has been a fusillade in our street (Roquépine). During part of last night we heard the distant cannon, the drum, the clarion, and the tocsin. This morning we were surrounded by National Guards, and we heard the fusillade in the direction of the Faubourg St. Honoré and Champs Elysées. After a while the fight was close to St. Augustin, in the Boulevard Malesherbes, and at last the soldiers reached our street. We could not even put our nose to the window without the risk of being struck by a ball. The soldiers are installed in the house next to our

chapel, and are firing in the direction of Rue
Neuve des Mathurins (in a line with our Rue
Roquépine on the other side of the Boulevard
Malesherbes). They are at the doorway and at
the windows of each story. You may imagine
the noise and confusion we hear outside. About
nine o'clock we had worship in our room; all in
the house were present, and we prayed earnestly
to God to aid us and prepare us for whatever
might happen. It is blessed to feel the presence
of God in the midst of danger. The door of the
shop immediately in front of us has been broken
in with a hatchet, I suppose because they would
not open it. I heard a poor wounded man utter
a cry, I peeped out from under our window shutters and saw him carried off. Shortly afterwards
a soldier was killed on the spot close to our
library. A litter was brought, and he was carried with all haste to the other side of the street,
as at that time the balls were falling only on our
side. Our *concierge* just opened the great door
of the chapel enough to give a bottle of wine to
the soldiers. An artilleryman at the corner of
the Rue d'Astorg (a street close by us) was
killed or badly wounded. At one o'clock I went
up to Mr. Cook's apartment. The noise was
even louder there than in the library. A ball
has just flattened itself against the balcony of
Mr. Gibson's apartment. I came down to the
library. The cannon rolled and the fusillade
continued, but it was impossible for us to know
which side had the upper hand. From time to
time we heard the grating of the mitrailleuses.
Shells were bursting, but we knew not whence

they came nor where they were falling. The noise is something terrible. Mrs. Gibson, when they were here yesterday, regretted that they were not all in Paris. If she were here to-day she would wish herself in Chantilly.

4 p.m.

The fusillade still continues. I hear the soldiers mounting the staircase of the next house. Mr. Bordage (the schoolmaster) has not come to-day. Doubtless he has been unable to make the journey from his apartment. None of us dares to go out. Happily, I laid in 4lb. of bread on Saturday. No one, however, has much appetite or the heart to eat. Our cry is, " Lord, have mercy upon us."

6 p.m.

The fusillade continues just outside my door. In the distance I heard the rattling of the mitrailleuses and the cannonade. A sapper has just been into the chapel and says that the troops have entered on different sides; that they have surrounded Paris, and that they are about to deliver us from the Commune. After having drunk a glass of wine he took his post at our chapel door and began firing in the direction of the Rue Neuve des Mathurins. It is quite a punishment to us to be all kept prisoners here without being able to put our heads outside. I have managed, however, to look out, and find to my sorrow that the door of another of the shops on the opposite side of the street has been broken in, the window-shutters broken, and the fragments scattered about the middle of the street. I hope they have put everything away, but I am in great fear that during the night the shop will be plundered.

10.30 p.m.

I have been very anxious to go and barricade the shop opposite that has been broken into, but I saw that it was utterly impossible. The balls whistled in the street. A sergeant has installed himself in the house, so I hope all will be safe. This evening all the inhabitants of the building met in Mr. Cook's apartment, and partook of a slight repast. Afterwards we had worship, and then stayed awhile to talk over the perils of the day. I am much fatigued, but have no wish to sleep. The fusillade has diminished in intensity, but the cannon still roars, and from time to time we hear the firing from the windows of the next house. The night is black and dark, the gas lamps are not lighted. What a day! How long it has seemed! And what anxiety! What will this night bring? Will it be deliverance? May God grant it! Shall we be able to stir out to-morrow without the risk of being killed? I am not able to judge, for I am not able to understand what has been passing in our street and what is the strategy of the troops. One of the soldiers, however, assured us that they would be masters of Paris to-night; but I do not see that they have stirred from our street. They are in force in the neighbouring street, Rue d'Astorg, and are sheltered at the side of the French Protestant Church opposite us.

Midnight.

Many balls have come whistling against our chapel, and we hear bombs passing over the building. We *feel* the uncertainty of life, and that our existence hangs on a thread which may be broken at any moment.

May 23.

God has kept us safely through the night. I slept a little about two o'clock, but was much agitated. The fusillade and cannonade continued throughout the night. The soldiers have been firing close to my bedroom. Bullets struck our house from a barricade close by Duval's, in the Rue Neuve des Mathurins. Mr. Bordage has succeeded in arriving here, and tells us that the army occupies Batignolles, Place Clichy, the St. Lazare Railway Station, &c. About three o'clock in the afternoon the firing slackened, and Mr. Cook and Mr. Bordage went out on the side already in the possession of the troops. At four o'clock there was a sharper fusillade than we had heard throughout the day. A company of soldiers, their commander in front, advanced to drive away the insurgents; they advanced at marching pace notwithstanding that balls were raining in the street. One bullet has just struck my window, pierced the glass, broken off a piece of stone in its course, and has fallen at the foot of my bureau. Splinters of glass fell upon the bureau itself. Happily I was not there. At five o'clock the soldiers had driven away the insurgents from the barricade, and we could put our noses outside. I saw several soldiers lying dead, and others wounded. Crossing the street I found the shops opposite a complete scene of confusion, and attempted to barricade the doors to save them from being plundered. At six o'clock the soldiers evacuated our street, and advanced towards the Madeleine, where there was a barricade, against which the troops have been firing with cannon from a barricade constructed near Potin's, across the Boulevard Malesherbes. At last they succeeded in taking the barricade near the Madeleine. About the same time Montmartre was taken. At seven o'clock, while I was at Mr. Cook's, the little servant of Madame Paris came in and told us the sad news that Madame Paris and her brother had both been killed. They were together in their apartment, and a ball came with such force as to pass through the brother, killing him on the spot, and then strike Madame Paris on the chest. She just uttered the words, "I am dead," and sank lifeless on the floor. We were all stunned with grief and sorrow. Madame Paris was one of the most earnest evangelists in Paris.

Wednesday, May 24.

Mr. Cook has passed the night with Mr. Paris, who is overwhelmed with grief. At nine o'clock Mr. Bordage and I mounted the tower. The Tuileries were in flames! The Rue Royale was burning, and other parts of Paris were on fire! The insurgents before retreating, have poured petroleum on the buildings and set them on fire. I trembled with horror. We went out into the boulevard. The house next to us at the corner of the boulevard has been much injured, all the windows broken, and the façade disfigured and broken by shells. I could weep without ceasing over the dead lying about in great numbers, the frightful ruins, the irreparable devastation. The Tuileries are only a smoking mass of ruins. A portion of the Louvre is also on fire. The monsters took care, in order to accomplish their purpose, to saturate the floors and the walls with petroleum. The noise of the cannon and mitrailleuses still continues. Fighting is going on in the direction of the Faubourg Montmartre. The insurgents have batteries on the Buttes Chaumont, which are throwing petroleum shells into the centre of Paris. The soldiers are now giving no quarter, but shoot all who are taken; hence the insurgents are fighting with the energy of despair. It is said the Hôtel de Ville is also on fire. This evening—at nine o'clock—what a shocking spectacle!—we beheld the sky apparently all on fire in the direction of the Rue de Rivoli and the Faubourg Montmartre. It is impossible to describe it. The flames rose towards heaven with terrible intensity. The Ministère des Finances is announced on fire. One would have supposed it was all Paris burning. Even at this distance we could feel the heat. With such a sight around us one could well imagine the destruction of Sodom and Gomorrah.

This evening we went out to dine with Mr. Bordage. Mr. Cook joined us just as we were going out. While Mr. Bordage and I were talking, Mr. Cook was arrested. He showed his

THE RED FLAG. 281

papers; but that was not enough, and they were about to conduct him away between two soldiers. A worthless concierge, half drunk, had said to the corporal, " You must take him; he's a disguised Englishman." Mr. Bordage and I both came up and bore our testimony as to who he was; and, as I had my "patente" in my pocket, they at length yielded, and set Mr. Cook at liberty. I wanted them to take the concierge for denouncing a person without any knowledge of him, but the rascal had disappeared. In the present state of public feeling there is no telling what might become of anyone arrested for complicity with the Commune.

All the lower part of the Boulevard Malesherbes is riddled with balls. We went to the Rue Royale. Some houses are still burning. Others have already fallen in. It is on the Faubourg St. Honoré side that most injury has been done. The Restaurant Weber is all in flames. They were forming the "chaine" to throw water upon the fire. The Maison de Nouveautés at the corner of the Faubourg is completely demolished. Dead bodies were lying in the middle of the street, under the branches of the trees cut down by the shells. The Rue St. Honoré in the neighourhood of the Place Vendôme has also been much damaged. Happily, the Place Vendôme was taken by the troops before the insurgents had time to set it on fire. We could not go into the Rue de Rivoli, for shells were whistling along the street, but from a neighbouring street we saw the Tuileries. It is nothing but a great heap of blazing ruins; the Pavillon d'Horloge has fallen in. The heat burns you even at a great distance. No one can go near to attempt to extinguish the flames. The insurgents are throwing petroleum shells upon the burning palace. As we were looking on in horror we saw smoke rising on the other side of the Seine. The Ministères on

Ministère de la Marine.

fire! Returning home with hearts filled with sorrow, we heard shells whistling overhead. In the Rue St. Roch a bomb burst behind us, and knocked down the corner of a house. As we reached our door a shell passed over the chapel, and fell probably in the Faubourg St. Honoré.

On entering his apartment last evening, M. Bordage saw that his window was broken. A ball had passed through and cut the candle on his table in two. If he had been there he would certainly have been wounded, if not killed. So both at home and outside we have been in great peril. Blessed be God who has safely kept us.

One o'clock.

It is specially the women who are setting fire to the houses. Many have been taken in the act and shot at once. All foreigners taken with arms in their hands, who cannot give satisfactory explanations, are shot. Some executions took place yesterday near the *Caserne Pépinière*, and in the Rue Godot de Mauroi. The fire in the Rue Royale is nearly extinguished. We shall now escape, unless a bomb should set fire to our quarter.

Evening.

I have been to see Mr. Paris in his great grief. He was sitting beside his two dead, overwhelmed with sorrow, but graciously sustained. A perfect calm is depicted on the face of Mme. Paris. Beautiful in death! The ball, which, as I have already said, passed through her brother before it struck her, passed through the heart or lungs and came out at the neck. Death was instantaneous. All the ordinary arrangements for funerals are put out of course. The administration is disorganised, and no hearse or funeral carriage is to be had. What is to be done? They are burying anywhere and everywhere.

Thursday, May 25.

At five o'clock this evening Mr. Cook and I went to the funeral of Madame Paris. There were many people assembled, and Mr. Cook conducted the service in a little courtyard. All were in tears. After waiting some time a sort of funeral cart arrived at the door—no hearse was to be had. The cart already contained three corpses, and was about to take up three more in the same street. We all counted on walking towards the Clichy Cemetery, but the announcement was made that no one, not even the husband, would be allowed to follow. The two coffins were lifted in, and the cart pursued its mournful way.

This evening we walked along the Rue Royale, &c. Some houses, spared before, are now on fire; the same in the Faubourg St. Honoré and the Rue Boissy d'Anglas. We were nearly pressed into the *chaine*, but there were more men than were needed, and all the pumping did not avail to assuage the fire. On different sides we see first a thick smoke, then a brilliant flame, with tongues of fire undulating towards the sky. The Grenier d'Abondance is in flames. Many houses, theatres, and churches are on fire. Those wretches are setting fire to the buildings, and destroying all in their power, even if they themselves perish in the burning. Pieces of burnt paper from the Ministère des Finances, *obligations, actions de rente,* &c., are flying about in all directions. No one can tell where this disaster will stop. We can hear the cannon and fusillading in the distance. They say that fighting is going on in the Faubourg St. Antoine, and that the troops are nearing Belleville. The detonations of the cannon are frightful. The Buttes Montmartre are firing on the Buttes Chaumont. Very bloody combats have taken place in the Faubourg Poissonnière. Prisoners have been taken in great numbers, and among

Arrestation de Pétroleuses.

them *pompiers* who have been caught throwing petroleum upon the flames instead of extinguishing them. Women and young children are also among the prisoners, who are marched off between two ranks of soldiers, armed with revolvers to shoot any one who attempts to escape. Many women have been taken throwing petroleum into the cellars, some in the Boulevard Malesherbes close to us. All who are caught in the act are immediately shot. We see dead bodies lying about in the streets, and breathe the exhalations arising from them. How the devil gloats over such scenes! These wretched people would not have God. Destruction and ruin have been their weapons. And what destruction! what ruin!

Friday, May 26.

It is raining fast this morning. So much the better. It will help to put out the fires, for they have been multiplying. I am overwhelmed with grief and anguish. Who would have said, when we suffered so much during the siege, that we should have to endure sorrows a thousand times more poignant?

Saturday, May 27.

The cannons of Montmartre (in the hands of the Government) are firing constantly. At intervals we hear the fusillade in the distance. More and more killed and wounded. We have been to the Place St. Georges, and saw the remnants of M. Thiers' house. Nothing remains but the thick outside walls above the first story. If reconstructed, it will have to be rebuilt from the very foundations. On returning I passed by the barrier Blanche, where a great combat took place. Several houses around are riddled with shells and balls; the same at the Place Clichy. In the Rue Godot de Mauroy all was prepared by the insurgents for burning the houses, but the troops advanced so quickly that they were obliged to fly without having accomplished their design. We walked to the Palais Royal. Two-thirds of it are burnt, the Pavilion in the centre, and the left wing at the side of Rue de Valois. The Library of the Louvre, which was opposite the Palais Royal, is burnt, but the stones are not demolished as at the Tuileries. Thanks to the energy displayed by the troops, the galleries of the Louvre are saved from the fire. At the other side of the Seine, the Rue de Bac is nothing but a heap of stones, which are still smoking. The whole street is blocked with crumbling ruins. The part of the Rue de Lille abutting on the Rue du Bac is all burnt. The walls of the Caserne Napoleon are still standing, but the interior is all burnt. We were stopped to aid at the pumps, but managed to escape. Passing by the quays, we saw that the magnificent buildings of the Conseil d'Etat, la Caisse des Dépôts et Consignations, la Cour des Comptes, la Légion d'Honneur are nothing but smoking masses of *débris*. We passed at the end of the Boulevard St. Germain, near the Palais Législatif. The side of the palace bears traces of shells and rifle balls, but the palace itself has not suffered much. The Place de la Concorde, however, on the side of the bridge, bears the marks of a terrible artillery combat. The beautiful gas-lamps are on the ground, the balustrades destroyed, the statues of the fountains are some without heads, others without arms, and all the broken pieces are scattered about the place *pêle mêle*. The statue of Lille is knocked down. The Ministère des Finances is burnt.

Men were at work demolishing the famous barricade at the corner of the Place de la Concorde and the Rue de Rivoli. It was impossible to cross the Rue Royale. Water was being thrown on the houses, which, one after another, fell in. The little Rue Royale Chapel, being low and lying behind, is said not to have suffered, not-

La Légion d'Honneur.

withstanding that the house in front is all burnt, and the house at the side has fallen in. We came home much saddened. In the evening we went out to see if the sister of our pastor, M. Dugand, who, with many others, had been imprisoned at St. Lazare, was safe. Our course lay along the Faubourg St. Honoré, which has not suffered much, except from the fall of shells. We found to our joy that M. Dugand's sister was again in her own house safe and well. She was one of six hundred imprisoned at St. Lazare. Daily the insurgents told them they were about to be shot. When the soldiers took the quarter they were immediately set at liberty. The other hostages have not been so fortunate. Many of them have been shot. We complained during the siege of want of light in the streets. Now the streets are sometimes completely lighted up by the glare of the fires. At other times it is very dark. Not a single gas-lamp is lighted, and there is no gas in the houses. I suppose the streets will remain in darkness until the gas-lamps are repaired.

Sunday Evening.

What a week since last Sunday! No week during the siege was anything to be compared with it. My heart has been full of anguish. This is Whit-Sunday. Oh that God may bestow on us abundantly the gift of the Holy Spirit! Then I do not despair of the resuscitation of France and of Paris. But men have not been willing to acknowledge the existence of God nor of the Holy Spirit. Hence the abyss of misery into which they have fallen. Madame Sabatier this morning gave us a good *déjeuner*, a roast with carrots. After we had finished she told us that it was a morsel of the horse of an insurgent commandant, which had been killed near her son's house. After breakfast I went to Taitbout Chapel and heard M. de Pressensé. He appeared wearied, and but little disposed to speak. Nevertheless, he showed very beautifully that the bible contains consolations for such times of trouble. He besought Christians to pray, and to endeavour to enlighten our fellow-citizens, that they may not any longer remain without God, and that so great a disaster may be repaired. Leaving the Taitbout Chapel, I met a company of prisoners passing along the Rue Lafayette. My heart beat violently on seeing these poor unfortunate creatures, bareheaded, coats turned inside out, and marching along between two ranks of cavaliers, who, carbine in hand, were ready to fire on any who attempted to make their escape. I was told there were five thousand of them. Among them were women and children, who sometimes were obliged to run to keep up with the rest, or they would have been trampled on by the horses. They were taken at the Buttes Chaumont yesterday and this morning. Most of them were of hideous look, yet I could not but compassionate them, notwithstanding their crimes. The crowd hooted them as they passed along. I was ready to say to the people around me—Do you think that you are less culpable than they? No; unless you repent and be converted. Gendarmes brought up the rear of the cortége. I returned home saddened, thinking of those poor wretched creatures, many of whom could not be reckoned responsible for the part they had taken.

M. Scheffer preached the sermon at our service at Rue Roquépine, and Mr. Cook administered the Lord's Supper. One of our people living near the Pantheon told us that every moment they were fearing that the Pantheon would be blown up, for they knew it was full of gunpowder. Thanks to the courage of a soldier, the Pantheon, with all the quarter, was saved. Seeing a man in sailor's clothes coming up from the crypt, and divining what he had been doing, the soldier rushed into the crypt, found a slow match on fire, put it out with his foot, and so prevented a dire catastrophe. I went out with Mr. Cook, and we saw a great crowd around the *Magasin du Printemps*. A revolver had been fired from one of the neighbouring houses at two artillery officers. One of them had only escaped death by means of a leathern purse in his pocket, which had deadened the ball. All the houses near were searched, and, it was said, an officer belonging to Dombrowski's staff, who went in and out of the house as if he belonged to the regular army, was arrested. This evening we had a delightful prayer-meeting. May God hear our prayers and grant us calm and peace!

Monday, May 29.

Mr. Cook has been trying to obtain a laissez passer to quit Paris so as to join his wife and family at Jersey, but he has not yet succeeded. No one is allowed to leave the city without a special order from M'Mahon. The insurrection is now completely at an end, and those of the insurgents who fought to the last have either been killed or taken prisoners.

From a member of our congregation living in the Rue de la Victoire we have received the following communication : May 26,—They fought all round our house from Monday morning to Tuesday evening. Our quarter was surrounded with barricades, one at least in each of the following streets: Rue de la Victoire, near the Faubourg Montmartre, Chaussée d'Antin, Rue Joubert, Rue Caumartin, Rue de Provence, Rue St. Georges, Rue Laffitte, Rue Lafayette. The barricade in the Chaussée d'Antin was large and strong, as may well be supposed from the fact that, although the soldiers began to fire upon it on Monday evening, it was not carried till Tuesday evening. You cannot imagine what it is to hear the cannon, mitrailleuses, and guns almost at one's door. The cannons of the troops were placed in the Square of the *Trinité*, near the church ; those of the insurgents behind the barricade at the corner of the Boulevards. The noise was frightful. Our house has been injured by the shells ; but, thank God, no lives have been lost. Several houses in the Chaussée d'Antin have been seriously damaged, the Church of the *Trinité* is injured both outside and inside. Numbers of insurgents who were taken were summarily shot in front of the church. I cannot tell you what joy we all felt when we saw the real French flag. The army was greatly applauded throughout our quarter ; cigars, wine and money were distributed to the soldiers ; and oranges and flowers thrown out at the windows. It was a horrible sight to see men and horses lying dead in almost every street ; there were eight in the Chaussée d'Antin, six in the Rue Caumartin, three in the Rue Joubert, and everywhere else in proportion. The army lost no men in our quarter; but as they advanced they had much more to suffer, as many of the people in the faubourgs were on the side of the Commune. Even the women fired from the windows, and threw paving-stones on the soldiers' heads; and some, dressed in men's clothes, fought behind the barricades. The army has been obliged to take Paris almost street by street, the insurgents leaving one barricade to run to the next. To-day they are fighting at Belleville, the Buttes Chaumont, and the Faubourg St. Antoine; and we hope that in a day or two all will be finished. A great number of the chiefs are already taken and shot. Thousands of the insurgents have been killed, and ten thousand taken prisoners. The wives of the insurgents, seeing that their husbands are lost, are revenging themselves by poisoning our poor soldiers, giving them wine in which they have put poison. We saw a woman in the Chaussée d'Antin yesterday, who has poisoned forty soldiers, taken to her home to be shot at the door of her house as an example. Fourteen women were shot this morning at the end of our street for the same cause. Six hundred women were taken prisoners yesterday, some of whom had been throwing petroleum into the cellars by the air-holes. Children behind them were throwing matches to light it. Thus several streets have been burnt. The insurgents have set fire to most of the principal monuments of the city. Some are burnt down; others are still burning."

Chantilly, June 1.

The pompiers from Chantilly have returned; and, headed by the tricolour flag, formed a procession through the town. They report that the fires are almost entirely extinguished, and say that it is heartrending to see the ruins, and that no one who has not seen it can have any idea of the desolation of the city. It is said that the way into Paris will be opened in a day or two, and then I shall be able to give you my own impressions.

Paris, June 3, 1871.

I have this day seen the ruins of Paris! Going along the Boulevard Magenta towards the Château d'Eau, we saw on the right and left of the street bullet-holes on the houses without number; corners of houses broken away, and walls pierced by shells, the iron-work of balustrades bent or twisted, windows broken and window-frames crushed. The general aspect of the street, looking along its whole length, is not much changed, but when you pass the houses one by one, and look at the details of the injury, it is sad to behold. We noted in passing that the top of the gable of the new façade of St. Laurent is broken in. From one of the windows of almost every house was suspended a tricolour flag, and such we found afterwards was the case in almost every street of Paris. They most abound in the aristocratic quarters. In the Rûe de Rivoli, Rue de la Paix, &c., &c., we saw a forest of flags. But they were not absent even from the "Red" districts, everyone now being anxious to show his decided preference for the proper Government. Some friends of mine told of a man who might be seen in the street during the reign of the Commune, in the dress of a National Guard, and might be heard advocating Communistic doctrines, and who, the day after the Versailles troops entered Paris, donned his ordinary civil costume and appeared at the door of his house with his hands in his pockets. This may account for some of the National Guard who are " not in Paris," and have neither been wounded nor killed.

Arrived at the Chateau d'Eau, we saw around us a complete scene of desolation. The Magasins Réunis gutted, houses in ruins, the beautiful fountains in front of the barracks destroyed, marks of shells and rifle shots on every hand. Men were hard at work demolishing the barricades, which were at the end of every street. This was one of the points where the fight was fiercest. Proceeding along the Boulevard Beaumarchais towards the Bastille, we noticed the various contrivances of each house—and the like is to be seen throughout Paris—for stopping completely the air-holes and entrances to the cellars, so as to prevent malicious persons from setting fire to the houses with petroleum. At the Bastille the ruin is frightful, whole houses having fallen in. Photographers were busy, so that those who cannot be eye-witnesses of the destruction will be able, by means of those faithful delineations, to form a good idea of the amount of mischief that has been done. Near the Bastille, along the canal, is the Grenier d'Abondance, an immense range of warehouses, 2,300 feet long, where was stored a portion of the corn which served as food supply for the people of Paris during the five months' siege. This large place is smoking ruin, only the bare walls standing. The great pile was still smoking, as were also some houses near. We made our way to Père la Chaise to see whether a little tomb in which we have a special interest had been injured. We passed by the Rue Sedaine, which bears marks of a terrible conflict, into the Boulevard Voltaire (formerly Prince Eugène). In front of the Mairie of the 11th Arrondissment one of the great rallying points of the insurgents, were heaps of knapsacks, straps, képis, scraps of clothing, &c. Ah! where were the poor fellows who had worn them? Turning into Rue de la Roquette, we met Marshal M'Mahon, probably returning rom the prison to his head-quarters. As we passed the point where two prisons of la Roquette and des Jeunes Détenus dismally confront each other, and meditated on the terrible events which have taken place during the last few days (it was here the Archbishop of Paris, the curé of the Madeleine, and others were shot), we saw a company of soldiers march out of the prison des Jeunes Détenus and form in rank and file in front of la Roquette. A good deal of interest was excited, and people were clustering around, but, lest we should unwillingly "assist" at the execution of some poor creatures, we pursued our way. Happily, we found our little tomb uninjured. Nor did we find nearly so much havoc in the Cemetery as we expected. Here and there, especially on the heights overlooking Paris, where the fiercest resistance was made, the tombs are chipped at the corners, and bear marks of rifle-shots; otherwise the Cemetery wears its usual appearance. A grand view of the city expands before you from the top of the hill above the chapel, which was remarkable to us from the absence of two prominent objects— the central tower of the Tuileries, and the top of the Hôtel de Ville. On our way to the interior of the city we passed again through the Place de la Bastille. The column in the centre of the Place, on the site of the old Bastille, is still erect and surmounted with the gilt figure, but the basement bears marks of a fire, and the interior, it is said, is burnt. Passing along the Rue St. Antoine, we observed right and left the marks of a hard street fight; the façades of the Church St. Antoine and another smaller church in the same street have been much damaged by the explosion of shells. Entering the Rue de Rivoli we met a respectably-dressed man, surrounded by soldiers, being marched off to prison. The poor fellow was deathly pale, and was probably as innocent as ourselves. We were now in front of the Hôtel de Ville, of which the walls alone remain. The older part in the centre has fallen in. Thankful were we to see the venerable pile of Notre Dame' intact. We next visited the Halles Centrales, which have been riddled with bullets. Entering St. Eustache, where we "assisted" three weeks ago at a club, we saw that the eastern stained-glass windows were much broken. The exterior of the church has also been damaged by bombs. Returning to the Rue de Rivoli, and continuing towards the Louvre, we were quite saddened by the sight of the houses on each side, completely

Place du Carrousel.

destroyed except the exterior walls. In some of the skeletons of apartments were to be seen mirrors and other articles of household furniture wonderfully spared in the midst of the general conflagration. At last we were before the Louvre, which happily was saved and bears only a few marks of shells. Through the Rue

de Rivoli gateway we entered the Place du
Carrousel, and gazed upon the *skeleton* of the
Tuileries. The *débris* was still smoking. Passing out by the new Grand Archway, which is
uninjured, we crossed the Seine, and passed the
Hôtel des Consignations, Palais du Quai d'Orsay,.
and the Palais de la Légion d'Honneur, of all

Fontaine. Place de la Concorde.

of which nothing remains but the outside walls.
We passed close by the Corps Législatif, the
façade of which has been much injured by shells,
and then into the Place de la Concorde. The
damage done in this incomparable square, although considerable, is *comparatively* small.
Here is a beautiful fountain almost destroyed,

there the statue of Lille broken down, and its head lying on the asphalt, here lamp-posts riven in twain, there the tail of one of the plaster-of-Paris horses at the entrance of the Tuileries Gardens knocked off; but, as you stand in the centre and look westward up the Champs Elysées to the Arc de Triomphe, northward towards the Madeleine, eastward towards the gardens of the Tuileries, and southward towards the Corps Législatif, you really miss nothing from the grand panorama but the Tour de l'Horloge of the Palace of the Tuileries. As you pass along the Rue Royale, after No. 10, up to which the houses are intact, havoc, ruin, and desolation stare you in the face. The houses at the corner of the Rue Faubourg St. Honoré, and one of the houses at the corner of Rue St. Honoré, are a mass of ruins, piteous to behold. Far up on a wall of the sixth story of one of the houses, all the rest of the building having fallen down, we could discern a dress and an umbrella hanging by nails, probably the property of some servant-maid, who had only just time to escape herself. No ruins in Paris are more complete than those of the Rue Royale, except those of the Rue du Bac. Madame de Stael would not now be able to say, if asked whether she did not much admire the surroundings of the Lake of Geneva, "Yes, but not so much as Rue du Bac!" We were very anxious to ascertain whether the little chapel in the Rue Royale had been injured, and made our way to it by the court behind. It is not damaged in the least! With houses in front and at the side on fire, it has escaped!

reminding one of the bush enveloped in flames, yet remaining unconsumed, or the three Hebrews who though "in the midst of fire" had "no hurt." The façade of the Madeleine bears deep traces of the combat which raged so fiercely in front of the building, some of the magnificent fluted Corinthian columns being seriously chipped. There was a hot fight along the Boulevard Malesherbes, and most of the houses bear traces of it; but No. 19 has suffered most, the third and fourth stories being completely covered with bullet-holes. The house at the corner of our Rue Roquépine has more than two hundred marks of rifle-shots upon it, and the lower story has been much knocked about, and the beautiful mirrors completely smashed. I counted thirty-two marks of bullets upon the façade and turrets of our chapel. One ball has broken a corner of one of the great windows and buried itself in the stone so deeply that it will doubtless remain for years a memento of the eventful days of May, 1871. One bullet came close to my study window and chipped off a piece of stone. Another dashed into our balcony close to the drawing-room window. Another broke through the roof into our attic.

We walked to the Place Vendôme. Strange to say, not a single house has been burnt in this centre of the insurgents, where their utmost vengeance was to have been wreaked. They were, without doubt, surprised, and had no time to carry out their nefarious design. We observed that the bronze has been almost entirely stripped off the stone, and the stones themselves separated and distributed about the centre of the square previous to the reconstruction of the monument. Passing along the Rue Castiglione into the Rue de Rivoli, we saw what was the Ministère des Finances a complete mass of ruins. Again crossing the Place de la Concorde, we examined particularly the obelisk to see if it had been at all injured. It seems to me that it must have been in the direct line of fire from the barricade at the end of the Rue de Rivoli; and yet not an injury has it received except a slight shell-mark on the granite basement containing the inscription, just above the word, "*antiquissimum*." "Four thousand years" and "the oldest monument but one in the world" commanded respect even from the insurgents!

Sunday, June 4.

Feeling a particular interest in the place in which I began my ministry in Paris nearly nine years ago, I went this morning to see if I could get into the Rue Royale Chapel, having seen the outside yesterday. I succeeded in entering and could not but thank God when I found that the place which has to so many Methodists such hallowed associations is all safe. Not a pane of glass has been broken, not a seat injured. The blessed sanctuary where William Toase preached for eleven years, where William Arthur and others ministered, and which, though it has passed into other hands, resounds with the same gospel, remains intact. May it long be a Bethel; and, saved as by fire, may it still be the birthplace of souls!

June 5.

The Champs Elysées, notwithstanding all the battering by shells, looks much the same. A few branches of trees have been torn down and a few lamp-posts injured, but the general effect is the same. The Arc de Triomphe, notwithstanding that it has received scores of shells and has some of its bas-reliefs damaged, looks almost uninjured. But many of the houses in the Avenue de la Grande Armée are almost in ruins, and the neighbourhood of the Porte Maillot is a desolation. We followed a crowd into a *Chapelle Ardente* of the Madeleine, and saw the coffin (draped in black velvet and covered with beautiful flowers) in which are the remains of the Abbé Deguerry; and at the Archevêché in the Rue Grenelle St. Germain we saw the Archbishop lying in state. The body has been embalmed and is dressed in gorgeous robes. The face did not look like death, but like a wax figure or what one imagines a mummy to have been. The interment is to take place on Wednesday next.

June 7.

In looking over our chapel to find other traces of the fierce conflict which raged in and around our street, I find a black mark on a stone ledge at the side of the principal entrance of the building, and, on inquiry, learn that a soldier who stood at our chapel-door for eight hours firing on the insurgents rested his gun upon this ledge to take aim and fire. On examining the façade of the chapel I find I understated last week the number of bullet marks it has received. The top of our turret seems to have been a special mark to aim at.

The new Church St. Augustin near us, in front of which there was a hard and long fight, has received on its façade and dome many marks of shells. Going into the interior, we found that many of the stained-glass windows had been shot through. Otherwise the church is not damaged. Entering the Madeleine, I discovered no trace whatever of the terrible combat which took place when, according to report, two or three hundred of the insurgents took refuge in the church, and were all of them shot or bayoneted. Not able to get into the Parc Monceau, the gates being locked, I walked around the beautiful enclosure which used to be my favourite place of recreating, speculating upon which might be the spot where so many poor wretches had been executed. We hear that many bodies dug up from the *fossés* near the barricade are to be brought here and burnt. Good-bye to the Parc Monceau for some time as a pleasure-garden. I am glad, however, that any place has been chosen for the incineration of the corpses, for Paris, in certain parts of the city, is not at all sweet just now. Whiffs of earthy odours of decomposition meet you here and there, especially near the quondam barricades, and a strong oily smell, which they say is not unhealthy, but certainly is sickening, tries your temper in the districts where houses have been burnt. The weather, fortunately, may I not say providentially, is cool, and an almost wintry wind is blowing over the city; otherwise we might expect a pestilence. As I pass over places where I saw deep trenches dug in front of the barricades three weeks ago, and now, from unmistakable signs, cannot fail to know that there are dead men underneath the newly-laid road, many passages of the Word come to my mind : " Whoso diggeth a pit shall fall therein." " The heathen are sunk down in the pit that they made ; in the net which they hid is their own foot taken." " But thou, O God, shalt bring them down into the pit of destruction ; bloody and deceitful men shall not live out half their days." It is a comfort to breathe freely again in Paris, and to feel some security for life and property, which one never did under the reign of the Commune. Yet never was a city more completely kept down by soldiery. Patrols march along the streets night and day, and no one is allowed to pass the gates of the city after nine o'clock at night. Nevertheless, Paris is reviving, commerce is returning, the streets are filling, orders for goods are coming in fast, and the Boulevards are almost as gay as ever. The city, phœnix-like, is springing up from its ashes. The trees have not, as in the Revolution of 1848, disappeared, but, although here and there branches have been lopped off, still grace the Boulevards with their bright green foliage.

Paris has now a grand chance—such a chance as a nation has never had—of rebuilding its principal monuments in the strength of its recuperative power. Most nations, which have had their chief buildings ruined, have had them destroyed when they have ceased to possess recuperative power. France, notwithstanding the heavy war indemnity, is rich still; and has the power and the wealth to rebuild her capital in a style more splendid than ever. Whether it is wise for a nation to spend money on magnificent buildings is a question, but nations have done it and will do it. One cannot but regret bitterly the wickedness which led to the firing of Paris, but as the result Paris may become grander than ever. Great cities owe much to great fires. What does not London owe to its great fire? What will not Constantinople owe to its great fire of eighteen months ago? As an Englishman proud of my country, I should not be sorry, provided it were not the work of incendiaries, and that in the burning not a single precious article or valuable paper were destroyed, if the whole line of buildings between the Bank and Charing-cross, including the Great Temple in the middle of St. Paul's Church-yard, were laid low. London, with her redundancy of wealth, would then build streets worthy of being the principal thoroughfare of the chief city of the world. I find a response, doubtless, in all but the reference to St. Paul's; but I am free to confess that Sir C. Wren is no favourite of mine. He has left as his legacy to the City of London some few mediocre churches, the disfigurement by the two western towers of the finest ecclesiastical building of which London boasts, Westminster Abbey, and a copy (said to be an improvement) of St. Peter's at Rome, which is a mixture of the features of a heathen temple and Mahommedan mosque. But London is not destined to have any such chance. Her fire-engines are such that there is no possibility of any fire spreading; and, if they had gone in any force to Paris, much that has been destroyed under the smouldering ruins might have been spared.

Now that we are all under the fresh impression of horror caused by the firing of Paris, and every one is hurling against the perpetrators of such a crime unmingled indignation, there is danger lest we should forget that there were three different kinds of supporters of the Commune. The first, those who *bona fide* wished only municipal liberties for Paris. Those who went so far only with the Commune, and were moderate in their views, will certainly sooner or later succeed.

"Freedom's battle, once begun,
Bequeathed from bleeding sire to son,
Though often lost, is surely won."

Others there were who were Communists because, under the teaching of the International Society, they were determined that capital should no longer tyrannise over labour. The First Revolution may be said to have been the struggle of the people against the nobles; this late revolution has been a struggle of the employed against the employers. "We want," say they, "a share of the profits."

A third kind were desperadoes, who wished to pull down every one higher than themselves; and in carrying out their designs were willing to undertake any desperate measure. For the last, who set fire to the public buildings, and employed women and children to pour petroleum into the houses, we can have no pity or compassion whatever. Yet one cannot but regret the indiscriminate brutal savagery of the soldiers during the first few days of their victory. One of our local preachers saw a man coolly pricked to death by a soldier, and then lifted up on the point of the bayonet for the inspection of the lookers on. No sympathy was evinced for the poor old man, and two ladies (?) suggested that the soldier should "chop the rat's head off!"

I observe in the streets of Paris the broad white caps of the "sisters," which for the last two months have been conspicuous by their absence, again flitting and flapping about; and the priests, who if seen at all, walked along with a downcast and dejected look, step out with a confident air and somewhat haughty mien. We are now almost certain to have a Monarchy again in France, and with a Monarchy, protectionist duties, priestcraft, &c., and the education of the people in the hands of the priests, which means a high education for the favoured few, and the bulk of the people kept in ignorance. But how is it, if there are so many primary schools in France as are reported in the year-books, that so many of the people are unable to read and write? The simple reason is that so the priests *will* it. They keep them ignorant under the show of instructing them. I have taken pains to inform myself upon this subject by talking with the people—"How is it that you cannot read or write; did you not go to school when a child?" "Oh, yes; but the priests kept me all the time learning Pater Nosters and Ave Marias; and so, after years at school, I left without knowing anything." Who will say that this was not done by the priests with a design of keeping the people ignorant, so that they may keep their hold on them? Indeed, I have met with numerous instances which have convinced me that the priests designedly keep the key of the door of the temple of knowledge in their own hands, that the people may come to them for instruction in all things, and may look up to them as having superior knowledge. In ordinary life you meet with some monsters, who, though instructed on certain subjects, will not tell you anything lest you should become as well-informed as they. This is the general conduct of the priests.

In the panoramic view of Paris, as seen from the top of our tower, I do not observe since the recent disasters the slightest difference, the Tuileries being hidden by the Madeleine, and the Hôtel de Ville by intervening buildings. The Napoleon statue in the Place Vendôme, which I miss so much, had disappeared from the view before the fall of the Commune.

There has been much excitement to-day about the burial of the Archbishop, and crowds of people have flocked into the city. The cab fare rose this morning to 5f. the course, and 8f. the hour. We saw the procession as it made its slow way along the quay. There was nothing gorgeous or splendid, as was expected. The impression produced by the hearse and its surroundings was that it was the funeral of some grand personage who had expressed a desire to be buried quietly, without pomp or show. What made it imposing was the number of troops who marched slowly to the sound of the muffled drum. The *cuirassiers*, with their martial bearing, as the restrained horses stepped gently along, added greatly to the impressiveness of the scene. Notre Dame was surrounded with a compact crowd. We did not even attempt to get near the building. But those who were fortunate enough to enter describe the service as one of great solemnity. The ceremony was performed by the Bishops of Meaux, Chalons-sur-Marne, Versailles, Bayeux, Nancy, and Pamiers. Marshal M'Mahon, Generals Vinoy, de Cissey, Trochu, Douay, Ladmirault, Changarnier, and the members of the Assembly "assisted." The body of the Archbishop remained exposed in the Cathedral during the middle of the day; and at three o'clock, while vespers were chanted, was laid in the vault of the Archbishops of Paris.

The remnants of the barricades are fast disappearing, and in a few days not a vestige of them will be seen. Nothing but two corners at the entrance of the Rue de la Paix, which the demolishers were carting away as quickly as possible, remained this morning of all the fortress-like surroundings of the Place Vendôme. Preparations were also rapidly advancing for the re-construction of the column. *Affiches* abound almost as much as in the days of the Commune; but, instead of dealing in a single line with great questions (as for example, the separation of the Church from the State), in the fashion to which we have become accustomed of late, some of them are headed "Armée de Versailles," and signed "M'Mahon;" others forbid the sale of petroleum, and order arms to be immediately delivered up.

The general aspect of the city is that of a rebound from stagnation and death to activity and life. There will be plenty of work for masons, carpenters, and glaziers for a long time to come. Foreigners are arriving in great numbers, and the hotels are filling fast. During the past two months, notwithstanding all that has been said about the Commune being sustained by the foreign element, Paris has had a peculiarly *French* appearance. It had become a rare thing to meet a foreigner, and especially an Englishman. Now the city is resuming its former cosmopolitan look.

Many regrets have I heard expressed that our central Methodist chapel was not in the Rue Royale, or in the Boulevard Malesherbes. Such regrets will probably now cease as, if it had been in the Boulevard, it would probably have been riddled with rifle-shots and partially destroyed by shells, and if in the Rue Royale, it might have been burnt to the ground.

June 8.

I have been to Asnières. The scene of ruin is such as no words can describe. The houses on the quays are most of them destroyed, the railway station has been entirely demolished;

but our little chapel, only a stone's-throw from the station, and not fifty yards from houses that have been pounded with bombs, has escaped with almost no injury at all. A few stones chipped off, a hole in the roof, and a window-sill smashed, we reckon nothing, compared with the surrounding devastation. God be praised for His care over His house!

Paris, June 14, 1871.

The great subject of conversation everywhere is the form of government which France is to have. Thiers' speech in the Assembly last Thursday is highly applauded, and Thiers himself is winning golden opinions. The most intelligent and well-informed are inclined to blame Thiers as indirectly the author of many of the misfortunes of France; but with the many who know not and do not care to inform themselves of the words and acts of the now Chief of the Executive for the last thirty or forty years, the present only is regarded, and Thiers is the man of the hour, getting more credit than he deserves. The Orleans Princes have paid their respects to Thiers at Versailles, and have met the Comte de Chambord at Dreux; and it is now generally understood that the programme is Thiers, Dictator for two years; then Henri V., the crown reverting at his death, as he has no issue, to the heir of the Orleans family.* But what meanwhile, of the Republic? A Republic is not possible in France, there being but few Republicans, and the French people not

---

* Public political opinion, never at one stay in Paris, has considerably changed since this letter was written.

being prepared for a Republic. In France, the Republic always forms the stepping-stone to a Monarchy or an Empire. Paris is fast filling with strangers who have come to see the ruins, but, their object accomplished, they take their departure. Business is very dull, and shopkeepers complain of the want of the rush of commerce which they expected along with the rush of strangers. Active measures are being taken to prevent the miasma which might have poisoned the air of the city during the hot months, if the corpses, hastily buried during that dreadful week between the 21st and 28th of May, had been allowed to remain where they were at first thrown. As I passed the Pont de la Concorde on Monday morning last, I saw grave-diggers exhuming the bodies from the quays, and two large vans in waiting to receive their putrid deposit and transport it to one of the Cemeteries. It is sad indeed to see occasionally a poor fellow marched off between soldiers, for search is still being made in the houses for hidden insurgents. On Sunday afternoon I saw a man looking the image of misery, walking in front of two mounted soldiers who followed with loaded rifles; and on Monday morning in the Rue St. Honoré I saw conducted by a soldier, a walking figure above whose shoulders there was nothing of the "human face divine," but a mass of bruised and swollen flesh covered with blood. My blood ran cold as I passed. The trifling remark of a Parisian who happentd to be near, and witnessed this sight of horror, was only an index of the general levity and frivolity of the inhabitants of the city. They have neither, so far as I can see, been humbled by the events of the war, nor saddened by the disasters which have befallen the city. *La Polichinelle*, (the French Punch and Judy) is as popular as ever, and the Boulevards are the Boulevards still.

It may comfort English people who are intending to take a trip to Paris to know that at present there is no epidemic in the city. The Commune, dirty as its adherents looked, has not left a legacy of disease, but has purged Paris of epidemics (and among them the small-pox) which have raged in the city for more than a year.

On Sunday afternoon last a very solemn and impressive funeral service took place at Asnières. The body of the poor woman who had acted as *concierge* of our chapel, and who had been killed in her cottage by a shell two or three weeks ago, was carried to its final resting place in the Courbevoie Cemetery. When the sad accident occurred bombs were raining in Asnières, so the disconsolate husband had to dig a "narrow house" in the little garden in front of the cottage, awaiting quieter times for a funeral service. It was intended to hold the service in the cottage, but so many had assembled that we were compelled to hold it in the open air. The sight as we neared the humble dwelling was one to be remembered. There, in front of the little garden wall, was the exhumed coffin, covered with a plain black cloth, and all around a numerous group of people, English and French, some friends of the deceased, others sympathisers with the bereaved family. Close by the garden gate was the sorrowing husband surrounded by the four motherless children. Behind was the cottage, with one side entirely broken in by the shell which killed the poor woman. All were impressed and solemnised, and some brushed away their tears during the service, in which the English Congregational minister in Paris (the Rev. T. Baron Hart) took part. The procession then moved slowly along, passing near the Château de Bécon, to the cemetery. Addresses both in French and English were delivered to the large company gathered around the grave; and as the poor woman, thus suddenly taken away, had a good hope of eternal life, all were comforted with the words, "Blessed are the dead which die in the Lord."

June 15.

I regret to find that the determination to seek to take their revenge sooner or later on Prussia is again manifesting itself among the Parisians. During the last two or three months the talk has all been about the Commune, but now you hear everywhere the expression of a resolve to bide their time for vengeance. And it is not, like the usual nervous utterances of Parisians, a flighty and enthusiastic expression, but the sullen and moody telling of a deeply-formed purpose, like a German or English resolve of revenge. Alas for France, and alas for the hope of the peace of Europe!

France is adopting, as every one from the beginning of the war foresaw would be the case, the Prussian system, and ordering compulsory military service for every Frenchman. This is, without doubt, the most disastrous result of the war, and will do more than anything else to throw back the civilisation of Europe. With a nation like Prussia, whose sons are stolid and phlegmatic, it is not dangerous to enforce military service, and make every man a soldier ; but with such an excitable nation as the French, universal instruction in the use of arms will be fraught with the greatest peril. High-spirited, proud, and susceptible, they will be always finding a *casus belli*, and good-bye to the idea of European peace ! German officers have again and again expressed to friends of mine their surprise to find that French people are not, as they supposed them, a military people ; that, instead of finding every French peasant burning with the military spirit, they have found them plodding along in blouses, anxious above all for peace, and to be allowed to pursue quietly their rustic life. All will be altered now ; and Germany, when within the next few years she again encounters France in arms, will find her a very different foe from the France of 1870 ; and who knows but that, before the end of this century, there may be a similar triumph in Paris to that which is now being celebrated in Berlin ? I vainly hoped that France would feel herself fairly beaten and be willing to accept her inferior position in Europe, regarding it as the result of what Frenchmen call *la force majeure*. But no ; wherever I go I hear the same language—a willingness to make any sacrifice, no matter how great, to be revenged on Prussia. They say, one and all, if peace had been made on reasonable terms after Sedan, France and Germany would have been friends; but now that Germany in the hour of her victory has imposed such hard terms of peace, a spirit of implacable hatred and revenge has been aroused, which can only be satisfied by an attempt at retaliation. It is most sadly ominous for the future that Parisians, borrowing a feature entirely foreign to themselves, but characteristic of the Germans ever since Tacitus wrote his graphic description of them in his "Germania," say gloomily that France must have her revenge, even if she should have to wait a century for it. Such is Europe in the nineteenth century of the Christian era!

One great subject of conversation in Paris is Trochu's speech in the Assembly. Parisians generally consider his cause not proven, and think that if the city had been fortunate enough to have a more energetic governor, things might have been very different. Napoleon I. used to say to his generals, "I will give you anything but time," and so succeeded. Trochu seems to have been impressed with the Arab motto, "There will be another day to-morrow," and so failed. In one point, however, Parisians entirely agree with Trochu, that the second siege was a natural sequence of the first, and that so the Germans were indirectly the cause of the excesses of the Commune.

The *Siècle* gives an instance of the summary execution of an innocent man (doubtless one out

of many) during that terrible week between the
21st and 28th of May :—

"Everybody remembered that several journals
announced the death of Billioray, member of
the Commune, arrested on the 26th May in the
Avenue la Bourdonnaye, and shot at the
Military School. It is now well known that
Billioray was not taken until a few days ago, and
that he is at Versailles awaiting his trial. Here
are the details of the execution of the poor
fellow who was the victim of his likeness to
Billioray. On the 26th of May, about half-past
two in the afternoon, an individual tolerably
well dressed, walking along the Avenue la
Bourdonnaye, was surrounded by a crowd shouting, 'It is Billioray, member of the Commune.'
A patrol of the 6th of the line, who happened
to be passing in that direction, arrested the so-
called Billioray, and conducted him to the
Military School. The crowd followed, shouting,
'It's Billioray.' The poor fellow protested, but
the shouts drowned his voice. The officer before
whom he was conducted, convinced of his
identity by so many witnesses, ordered his immediate execution. 'But I swear that I am not
Billioray,' said the unfortunate man, 'I am
Constant, and live very near here, at Gros-
Caillou; go and ask my neighbours.' 'He is
lying, the coward,' vociferated the bystanders;
'he is Billioray, we're sure.' And a crowd of
people who had never in their lives seen the
member of the Commune, cried aloud, 'It's
Billioray.' The officer gave the order to execute
the poor man, who struggling in vain, was seized

and shot at once. In the evening the body, with many others, was sent to Issy to be buried. Now that the true Billioray is arrested, the sad and fatal mistake is sufficiently evident, and papers, found upon the unfortunate man who was shot, prove that his name was really Constant, and that he was an honourable citizen, a father of a family, and a hosier by trade, who had taken no part whatever in the politics of the day."

Last evening there was a gathering of representatives of the English in Paris at the Cercle des Chemins-de-fer in the Rue Michaudière to do honour to the Rev. Dr. Smyth, who has remained unflinchingly at his post in the English Church, Avenue Marbeuf, during the two sieges, and is now about to leave Paris. Lord Lyons and two of the secretaries of the British Embassy were present; the medical profession was represented by Drs. Herbert, Shrimpton, and Cormack; and the English churches, the Congregational and Wesleyan chapels, by their respective ministers. According to the wont of Englishmen, we dined together, and many were the good wishes expressed for the future happiness and welfare of the honoured clergyman, whose name will long be remembered with affection by the English poor in Paris.

Frenchmen, although fully aware of the great burden they must bear through increased taxation for many years, are full of hope that their country will easily get over its financial difficulties. France is one of the richest countries in Europe, and can bear a heavy taxation. It is a question for time to settle how far the restoration of protectionist duties will hinder its commercial prosperity. In ordinary years France grows enough corn and more than enough wine and oil for its inhabitants. Its best wines, silks, and *articles de Paris* other nations *will* have at whatever cost. A few years of peace, and France will have righted herself.

P.S.—April 11th, 1872. Subsequent events have justified every one's expectations. France is not dead nor dying. Although scarcely a year has elapsed, she is really stronger to-day than before the war. Her return to prosperity, in so short a time, after events so disastrous, is simply marvellous. Oh that in her returning prosperity she may remember God !

I have preferred to reprint these letters just as they appeared in the " Watchman," resisting the strong temptation to remodel them in the light which has since been thrown upon so important and eventful an episode in French history. The only alteration is in Mr. Jonathan Holden's account of his escape from Paris after its investment by the German army, which is here given in his own words. W. G.

www.ingramcontent.com/pod-product-compliance
Lightning Source LLC
Chambersburg PA
CBHW030017240426
43672CB00007B/995